VOICES FROM AN EARLY AMERICAN CONVENT

VOICES FROM
AN EARLY AMERICAN
CONVENT

Marie Madeleine Hachard and
the New Orleans Ursulines,
1727–1760

EDITED BY EMILY CLARK

LOUISIANA STATE UNIVERSITY PRESS
BATON ROUGE

Published by Louisiana State University Press
Copyright © 2007 by Louisiana State University Press
All rights reserved
Manufactured in the United States of America
Louisiana paperback edition, 2009

DESIGNER: Melanie O'Quinn Samaha
TYPEFACE: Adobe Garamond Pro
TYPESETTER: G&S Typesetters, Inc.

LIBRARY OF CONGRESS CATALOGING-IN-PUBLICATION DATA

Hachard, Marie-Madeleine, d. 1760.
  [Relation du voyage des dames religieuses Ursulines de Rouen à la Nouvelle-Orléans. English]
  Voices from an early American convent : Marie Madeleine Hachard and the New Orleans Ursulines, 1727–1760 / edited by Emily Clark.
     p. cm.
  Includes index.
  ISBN-13: 978-0-8071-3237-1 (cloth : alk. paper)
  1. Hachard, Marie-Madeleine, d. 1760—Correspondence. 2. Ursulines of New Orleans (New Orleans, La.)—Biography. 3. Ursulines—Louisiana—New Orleans—History. 4. New Orleans (La.)—Church history. I. Clark, Emily, 1954– II. Title.
  BX4705.H13A413 2007
  271'.97402—dc22
  [B]

                                                              2006031609
  ISBN-13: 978-0-8071-3446-7 (pbk.)

CONTENTS

ACKNOWLEDGMENTS

This book represents the contributions of many people, my own the least among them. Five eighteenth-century Ursuline nuns first committed to paper the words that constitute the substance of this volume. My largest debt is to these extraordinary chroniclers of a largely unknown chapter in early American womanhood: Marie Madeleine Hachard, Marie Tranchepain, Marguerite Judde, Marguerite Bernard de St. Martin, and Perinne Elizabeth Bellaire. Two gifted linguists, Maria Dolores Hernandez, O.S.U., and Jane Frances Heaney, O.S.U, both now deceased, crafted excellent translations of Hachard's letters and of the procession account of 1734. Heaney's translation of the procession account is reprinted here verbatim as it was published in her monograph, *A Century of Pioneering: A History of the Ursuline Nuns in New Orleans, 1727–1827,* edited by Mary Ethel Booker Siefken and published in 1993 by the Ursuline Sisters of New Orleans. I substantially edited Hernandez's manuscript translation, but the work remains largely hers. The

Ursuline Sisters of New Orleans hold the copyright to both translations, and I am grateful to them for allowing me to use them as the foundation for this volume. This project developed over a rather long period of time, during which three different prioresses of the Ursuline Sisters of New Orleans gave me their support in both formal and informal ways. It is my pleasure to thank Esther Redman, O.S.U.; Carla Dolce, O.S.U.; and Carolyn Marie Brockland, O.S.U. The Archives Nationales de France, Historic New Orleans Collection, Newberry Library, and New York Public Library generously granted permission to reproduce maps and illustrations in their collections.

As a historian, I took on the role of translator and editor with no small trepidation. I thank Mary Laven and Peter Bailey at the University of Cambridge for good counsel and encouragement, and especially the anonymous reader for the Press, who helped me give Marie Hachard and her sisters in religion the introductions they deserved. Sophie White at the University of Notre Dame helped me decipher some particularly tricky passages in badly deteriorated manuscripts. The editorial staff at Louisiana State University Press has been wonderfully supportive of this project from its inception. I especially thank Rand Dotson and Cynthia Williams for shepherding the manuscript so expertly through the publication process. Any faults that remain are mine alone.

Sylvia Frey, Michael Kane, Joan Kay, Diana Pinckley, John Pope, and Marianne Wafer have always been willing to hear my stories about the Ursulines and have helped me to see them in new ways. I thank Ron Biava for his love and his insistence that Hurricane Katrina not be allowed to derail this project.

My biggest debt to a living Ursuline is to Joan Marie Aycock, O.S.U., archivist for the New Orleans Ursulines, to whom I owe my acquaintance with her colonial predecessors. When she gave me access to the manuscript materials held in her community's private archives, she opened a door onto a largely hidden past filled with treasures for scholars and students of the history of women, religion, and race. She also introduced me, with warmth and humor, to the contemporary world of convent and nun, a place far stranger than the eighteenth century for the inexperienced non-Catholic who turned up at her archive door a decade ago. I am happy that the publication of this volume gives me an opportunity to thank her publicly for turning the key in the convent gate and inviting me in to look around.

VOICES FROM AN EARLY AMERICAN CONVENT

THE DOCUMENTS

On a February day in 1727 a genteel young Frenchwoman was hauled unceremoniously by rope and pulley up the side of a sailing ship anchored in the harbor of the French port of Lorient to join an intrepid band of missionaries and colonists bound for Louisiana. At twenty years of age she was the youngest of twelve Ursuline nuns who were turning their backs on the predictable comforts of religious life in France to answer God's call to labor in the wilderness of the Lower Mississippi Valley. The young woman's name was Marie Madeleine Hachard. Because she was not yet a fully professed nun when she set out on her adventure, she had the freedom to maintain contact with her biological family. A dutiful daughter, she took advantage of that liberty to write a series of five letters to her father, Jacques Hachard, an official in the bureau of accounts in Rouen.

Marie Madeleine Hachard's letters describe the young

nun's journey from the bosom of her family to the shores of the Mississippi in an unaffected voice suffused with equal measures of excitement and religious idealism. Her letters regale us with narratives of adventure and the exotic from a perspective rare in eighteenth-century sources. Hachard's gender and her youth render her richly detailed account distinctive. She casts a keen eye over features of the environment and human nature that did not attract the attention of the official male voices that dominate the historical record for colonial Louisiana, offering a fresh perspective that makes for compelling reading.

Hachard's letters were originally published by her father in her hometown of Rouen in 1728 under the title *Relation du voyage des dames religieuses Ursulines (Relation of the voyage of the Ursuline nuns)*. Several other French editions appeared in the nineteenth and twentieth centuries. It was not until 1974 that an English translation of all five letters appeared in book form, privately published in a small run.[1] The sporadic publication of the letters and their limited availability in English have left them mostly unknown to the American readers who constitute their natural audience today. This new translated edition of Hachard's letters is intended to make this engaging source widely available to English-speaking students and historians.

A small selection of writings by other New Orleans Ursulines who were Hachard's contemporaries is included in this volume to complement her account. The obituaries of six of the founding sisters who remained in New Orleans until their deaths offer fascinating portraits of some of America's earli-

---

1. See appendix for publication history.

est missionary women. There is the mother superior, Marie Tranchepain, a Huguenot convert whose iron will was the bane of colonial administrators. Instead of the docile compliance they might have expected of a pious woman vowed to obedience, they encountered in her a determined leader who eschewed polite rhetoric in favor of clarity and bite. "I have never understood that the Company [of the Indies] had it in mind that our conduct would be subject to its orders . . . I would have had to be mad to accept such a condition," she wrote to the colony's ecclesiastical director in 1728 after civil officials had attempted to tell the nuns how to order their affairs.[2] And there is Cécile Cavalier, who had a "boundless zeal" for evangelizing enslaved women and girls. When she died, some from among those whom she had converted took up a collection to have masses said for her soul.[3] The section closes with the obituary of Hachard herself, revealing the family tensions that could arise over religious vocations in even the most pious households. Hachard's parents and siblings were notably devout. Of seven living children known from her letters, five either were in holy orders or were postulants. Nevertheless, Hachard's father, a city official of solid bourgeois rank, hoped that his young daughter would marry and not follow her older siblings into religious life.[4] He and the girl's mother were particularly distraught at

2. Archives des Colonies, Correspondance Général, Louisiane, Archives Nationales de France, Series C13A, hereafter AC, C13A, 11:279.

3. "Lettres circulaires," Ursuline Convent of New Orleans Archives, 212.

4. From Marie Madeleine Hachard's letters, we can reconstruct a family of seven living children, of whom five were either in religious orders or considering religious life. In addition to herself, she mentions on page 38 an unnamed brother who is

their daughter's plan to join a mission so far away from them. The obituary endows many of the passages in Hachard's letters with a larger human context, revealing the poignancy, as well as the pride, in her father's decision to publish his daughter's words. Taken together, these biographical sketches, written by the nuns to inspire those who followed, allow us to know how the female ideal was imagined by women themselves in an era when most writing on feminine virtue was produced by men.

Finally, there is an eyewitness account of the first public Eucharistic procession to take place in New Orleans, a grand and festive parade staged in 1734 by the nuns and the women and girls of the city to mark the completion of a new convent. Here the women of the frontier settlement take center stage with great ceremony, deploying the symbolism of religious myth to remind the inhabitants of the centrality of religion to civilized society and to assert women's importance in the work of God and his church.

Together, the letters of Marie Madeleine Hachard and the writings produced by her contemporaries at the New Orleans convent offer rare female perspectives on early American life. While these nuns obviously cannot be considered representative of the women who settled Louisiana, they often chose to

---

a religious; on pages 37 and 91 an unnamed sister who was a Franciscan is mentioned, together with a sister named Elizabeth who appears to have been a postulant or novice at the same convent; and on page 37 she mentions a sister named Louison who was a postulant at the Ursuline convent at Val-de-Grace. Marie Madeleine expresses her hopes on page 37 that another unnamed brother studying sciences would become a Jesuit. Only a sister named Dorothy, mentioned on page 38, did Hachard not link to religious life.

write of events and people who are otherwise invisible in the historical record. In doing so, they broaden our understanding of colonial life and offer precious glimpses of how women perceived and judged the eighteenth-century world around them.

When Marie Madeleine Hachard and her Ursuline companions set out for Louisiana, the boundary between the Old World and the new was only one of many they crossed. Other women who left France for the colonies did so as direct subjects of male authority, as wives—or future wives—daughters, or servants. The nuns went as free agents, a corporate community subject to the authority of their order's rule but obliged to male civil authority only by the limited terms of their business contract with the colonial proprietors. They earned and managed their own money and governed themselves according to their understanding of what God, not man, had called them to do in the colony.

In the strongly patriarchal society of eighteenth-century France, such women represented a paradox. Indisputably feminine, they sidestepped the roles of wife and mother that essentially defined their gender and eluded the male authority to which those roles were subject. They achieved their alternative femininity and found a measure of acceptance for it through a confluence of circumstances particular to early seventeenth-century France. As those circumstances altered over time and tolerance for their peculiar mode of femininity diminished, they sustained it largely by virtue of their own determination and ingenuity and the force of their moral conviction. Marie Madeleine Hachard's is part of that larger story of the Ursuline order's origins and early history.

Modern nuns run the gamut from cloistered contemplatives garbed in traditional habits to streetwise social activists in blue jeans living among the poor they serve. It was not always thus. The first nuns were female monastics who lived in community and emulated the ascetic life of silence, prayer, and bodily mortification led by the desert hermit monks of the early Church. Monasticism made its way to northern Europe in the sixth century, took root, and grew into one of the most well-recognized features of the medieval world. Monks and nuns lived in enclosed communities, their days consumed in long periods of prayer and much briefer intervals of study and work within their compounds. The medieval nun was a cloistered contemplative. She spent her days closed off from the outside world and from those for whose salvation she prayed.[5]

5. On female monasticism prior to the Reformation, see Lina Eckenstein, *Woman under Monasticism: Chapters on Saint-Lore and Convent Life between* A.D. *500 and* A.D. *1500* (Cambridge: Cambridge University Press, 1896); C. H. Lawrence, *Medieval Monasticism: Forms of Religious Life in Western Europe in the Middle Ages* (New York: Longman, 1984); Jo Ann Kay McNamara, *Sisters in Arms: Catholic Nuns through Two Millennia* (Cambridge, MA: Harvard University Press, 1996); and Patricia Ranft, *Women and the Religious Life in Premodern Europe* (New York: St. Martin's Press, 1996).

The activist, apostolic nuns of twentieth- and early twenty-first-century America succeeded a nineteenth-century flowering of Catholic women religious that was itself indebted to an expansion of the French apostolic model to other parts of Europe, particularly Ireland and Germany. For more on these teaching and nursing

When Protestantism challenged Catholicism in the sixteenth century, remnant Catholic female monasticism had only prayer as a weapon against the Lutheran incursion. By the end of the century, however, a new congregation of religious women, the Ursulines, was gaining a toehold in southern France. Named for St. Ursula, an early Christian martyr commemorated as the first female missionary, the Ursulines mounted a campaign of internal conversion that regained ground lost to the Protestant Huguenots of the sixteenth century. The order went on to become a bulwark of Counter-Reformation France in the early decades of the seventeenth century.[6]

The Ursuline apostolate that flowered in seventeenth-century France represented a radical departure from traditional cloistered convent life. Ursulines advanced the cause of religion not merely through their individual piety but through an active ministry that brought them into contact with the world. They worked to change human society through interaction with it, and their innovative strategy was one that made women the agents of religious propagation. Arguing that mothers are children's first and most important teachers, Ursulines devel-

sisters, see Carol K. Coburn and Martha Smith, *Spirited Lives: How Nuns Shaped Catholic Culture and American Life, 1836–1920* (Chapel Hill: University of North Carolina Press, 1999); Mary Ewens, *The Role of the Nun in Nineteenth-Century America* (Salem, NH: Ayer Company, 1984); Kathleen Healy, ed., *Sisters of Mercy: Spirituality in America, 1843–1900* (New York: Paulist Press, 1992); and Barbara Misner, *"Highly Respectable and Accomplished Ladies": Catholic Women Religious in America, 1790–1850* (New York: Garland, 1988).

6. Teresa Ledochowska, *Angela Merici and the Company of St. Ursula according to the Historical Documents*, trans. Mary Teresa Neylan (Rome: Ancora, 1967), 30–41; Elizabeth Rapley, *The Dévotes: Women and Church in Seventeenth-Century France* (Montreal: McGill-Queen's University Press, 1990), 48, 51.

oped a rationale for universal female education. In cities and towns throughout France, they built schools to educate girls of all social strata to ensure the survival and propagation of Catholicism through mothers properly prepared to form their children's faith.[7]

France's colonization of North America inaugurated a new phase in female religious life. A widowed mother from Tours named Marie Guyart turned her back on a successful secular life and motherhood to become an Ursuline. Inspired by the example of Jesuit missions to convert the Indians of New France, in 1639 she traveled to Quebec to found the first convent in French colonial America. Under her religious name, Marie of the Incarnation, she penned a series of letters in the 1660s to her grown son, himself now a priest in France. For the first time a female voice echoed the dramatic Jesuit accounts of Indian conversion that had been flooding France for decades, and pious young women were infected by Guyart's missionary zeal. Inspired by Marie of the Incarnation, young women joining the Ursulines in the closing years of the seventeenth century and the opening decades of the eighteenth often harbored an intense desire to cross the Atlantic in the cause of Indian conversion.[8]

7. Linda Lierheimer, "Female Eloquence and Maternal Ministry: The Apostolate of Ursuline Nuns in Seventeenth-Century France" (Ph.D. diss., Princeton University, 1994); and Rapley, *The Dévotes,* are the best English-language sources on the first generation of French Ursulines.

8. Leslie Choquette, "'Ces amazones du grand dieu': Women and Mission in Seventeenth-Century Canada," *French Historical Studies* 17, no. 3 (Spring 1992): 632; Marie de l'Incarnation, *Word from New France: The Selected Letters of Marie de l'Incarnation,* ed. and trans. Joyce Marshall (Toronto: Oxford University Press, 1967),

As a young convert from Protestantism, Marie Tranche-pain entered the Ursuline convent at Rouen in the last year of the seventeenth century. Like many of her contemporaries, she dreamed of being a missionary to the New World. But the convents in New France were small and could take only a few of the French nuns who wanted to join in the work of Indian conversion. Marie Tranchepain's was a futile aspiration until, in middle age, "God made known to her that a Jesuit, whom she did not know and who did not know her, but who was then in France, was to be her guide and leader in a foreign land where He wished her to serve Him by establishing an Ursuline Convent."[9] When a Jesuit missionary, Ignace-Nicholas de Beaubois, called on the Ursuline convent of Rouen in 1726 to propose a Louisiana mission, Marie Tranchepain believed God had answered her prayers. Less than a year later, joined by Marie Madeleine Hachard and ten others, she set sail for New Orleans.

THE SETTING

The French crown established Louisiana as a colony in 1699 to secure its claim to the Mississippi Valley against the English and Spanish, who had advanced on the Carolinas and Florida,

---

337. For a general description of the educational program of the Ursuline mission to Quebec in the seventeenth century, see Vincent Grégoire, "L'éducation des filles au couvent des Ursulines de Québec à l'époque de Marie de l'Incarnation (1639–1672)," *Seventeenth-Century French Studies* 17 (1995): 87–98.

9. AC, C13A, 10:67; "Lettres circulaires," Ursuline Convent of New Orleans Archives, 207.

respectively, and were beginning to extend their sights westward.[10] Early settlements on the Gulf Coast at Biloxi and Mobile Bay, under the command of the French Canadian Pierre Le Moyne and his brother Jean Baptiste, struggled to survive, let alone prosper. More a congeries of military outposts than a colony, early Louisiana was plagued by difficult Indian relations, an inhospitable climate, disease, poor soil, and a preponderance of unruly male inhabitants. A severe paucity of French-born wives discouraged the development of the sort of settled farming communities that would have brought a degree of stability and the outlines of French cultural and social order. More than a few colonists entered into relationships with Indian women and were drawn into the fur trade and other backwoods activities better adapted to sustaining these intimate partnerships, further frustrating the agricultural ambitions of colonial officials. The colony languished, showing no signs of developing the kind of staple crop economy that undergirded the flourishing English colonies in the Chesapeake and Carolina Lowcountry, whose tobacco and rice enriched the British Empire.

10. This section on French colonial Louisiana is based largely on Marcel Giraud, *A History of French Louisiana*, vol. 5, *The Company of the Indies, 1723–1731*, trans. Brian Pearce (Baton Rouge: Louisiana State University Press, 1991); Gwendolyn Midlo Hall, *Africans in Colonial Louisiana: The Development of Afro-Creole Culture in the Eighteenth Century* (Baton Rouge: Louisiana State University Press, 1992), 2–27, 57–155; and Daniel H. Usner Jr., *Indians, Settlers, and Slaves in a Frontier Exchange Economy: The Lower Mississippi Valley before 1783* (Chapel Hill: University of North Carolina Press, 1992). The best comparison of colonial Louisiana with the Chesapeake and the Carolina Lowcountry is provided by Ira Berlin, *Many Thousands Gone: The First Two Centuries of Slavery in North America* (Cambridge, MA: Belknap Press of Harvard University Press, 1998).

After an unhappy interlude under the faltering governance of an entrepreneurial proprietor, Antoine Crozat (1712–1717), Louisiana improved somewhat. In 1717, proprietorship was transferred to the Company of the West, reorganized as the Company of the Indies in 1718 by the Scottish-born French financier, John Law. Law proposed to jump-start the colony's development through investment and a bold scheme to increase its population. Under his direction, the Company of the Indies made large land grants to a limited number of wealthy concessionaires who hoped to transform their colonial lands into wildly profitable staple crop plantations. In addition to the laborers and artisans the concessionaires sent or brought with them to man their plantation enterprises, Louisiana was peopled with a large number of forced immigrants. Nearly thirteen hundred convicts, debtors, and petty criminals found themselves exiled and bound for Louisiana between 1717 and 1721. During the same years, ships bore nearly two thousand captives from Africa to slavery in the colony.

Law succeeded in building Louisiana's population from about four hundred French men, women, and children in 1717 to a diverse population of over seven thousand French and enslaved African inhabitants in 1721. This demographic triumph, however, did not translate into economic prosperity. The tobacco and indigo grown on Louisiana's plantations were of insufficient quality to compete with the products of the Chesapeake, South Carolina, and Caribbean. Nor were attempts to identify a successful alternative product, such as silk, successful. Law's investment bubble burst in 1721, high mortality diminished the population, and in 1723 a group of pragmatic bureaucrats were dispatched to Louisiana by the French directors of the Company of the Indies to salvage what they could of the disappointing enterprise.

During the Law years, the colony gained a permanent capital, New Orleans, which became its social, economic, and military focus. The city was founded in 1718 on the banks of the Mississippi River, a location deemed healthier and more easily defended than the coastal settlements that had preceded it. The embryonic city was laid out by a French engineer in an orderly grid and by the mid-1720s boasted a number of substantial official buildings, including a prefecture, prison, barracks, church, and military hospital. In addition to the socially marginal survivors of Law's French deportation scheme and a population of enslaved Africans, the city developed a concentration of skilled laborers and artisans as the concessionary plantations upriver failed, owing to a mixture of mortality from fever, supply shortages, unstable Indian relations, and disappointing results in staple crop cultivation. New Orleans was also, crucially, the colony's military headquarters. Louisiana could only survive if it successfully negotiated the dual and often entwined threats posed by hostile Indians and the British, who were increasingly their most dangerous rivals for dominance in the southeastern American mainland. The troops occupying the garrisons strung along the banks of the lower Mississippi were among the colony's most valuable resources.

These troops were uppermost in the mind of newly arrived colonial administrator Jacques Delachaise when he wrote despondently to the directors of the Company of the Indies about the state of the colony he had been sent to govern. "If you could, Gentlemen, induce four good gray sisters to come and settle here and take care of the sick, it would be much better," he pled in 1723.[11] Mortality in the capital's military hospital was desperately high, a liability that compromised Delachaise's chances of wresting personal professional success from his colonial posting. New Orleans's lingering population of exiled convicts, petty criminals, and sexually licentious women probably also suggested to Delachaise an additional advantage to the presence of hospitalier sisters, since in France they also often provided reformatory care for the socially deviant.

Unhappily for Delachaise, the Daughters of Charity who customarily managed public hospitals were in such high demand in France that none could be persuaded to take on the Louisiana project. His failure provided opportunities for two frustrated missionaries, the Jesuit superior for Louisiana, Ignace-Nicholas de Beaubois, and the Ursuline nun who would become the founding superior of the New Orleans convent, Marie Tranchepain.

The Jesuits were the celebrities of the French missionary world by the middle of the seventeenth century, and de Beaubois expected an enthusiastic welcome from colonial officials when he proposed an extension of their missionary activity into the new territory of Louisiana. Jesuits were lionized by the French public for their heroic exploits among the Indians of New France, which the society publicized in a multivolume series packed with hair-raising stories of martyrdom and near martyrdom at the hands of the "savages" who were the objects

11. AC, C13A, 7:20.

of their missionary efforts. Some officials, however, deemed the Jesuits too independent and aggressive to be good members of a colonial administrative team. When the Company of the Indies reorganized the administration of Louisiana in 1723, they snubbed the Jesuits and authorized the Franciscan Capuchins to provide clerical services to the new colonial capital of New Orleans and its vicinity. The Jesuit superior, who believed that the organization of a missionary school in New Orleans and multiple missions among regional Indians were beyond the capacity of the Capuchins, was advised that his order had been allocated the less crucial missionary field to the north of the capital.[12]

Ignace-Nicholas de Beaubois was disposed neither by his personality nor his background to accept the rejection of his aspirations without a fight. Born in France in 1689, de Beaubois entered the Jesuit novitiate at the age of seventeen. He was serving at the Kaskaskia mission in the French Illinois country in the early 1720s when he made a play for a larger role in the budding colonial enterprise in the Lower Mississippi Valley. By all accounts, he was talented, charismatic, and despite his youth, boldly assertive. One of the proprietary officials in New Orleans praised de Beaubois's intelligence and noted that people were "charmed by his preaching" and that "in spite of seven or eight years among the savages" he remained gracious and mannerly.[13] The young priest resolved quickly to apply both

12. The discussion of Ignace-Nicholas de Beaubois is largely drawn from Charles Edwards O'Neill, *Church and State in French Colonial Louisiana: Policy and Politics to 1732* (New Haven, CT: Yale University Press, 1966), 130, 160–75.

13. O'Neill, *Church and State*, 160.

his intellect and his charm, taking passage on a ship to France to plead in person before the directors of the Company of the Indies the cause of what he believed was the necessary course of missionary activity in Louisiana.

In Paris, however, de Beaubois infuriated company officials with his arrogant lecturing on proper missionary policy and his list of demands for the terms of a Jesuit contract with the company for clerical services. At one point they broke off talks with him and were willing to exclude the Jesuits from missionary work in the colony altogether. When tempers cooled, a compromise was negotiated, and de Beaubois made a peace offering that both curried favor with the proprietors and allowed him to advance the Jesuits' educational agenda in Louisiana. He proposed that, since Daughters of Charity were unwilling to accept charge of the hospital in New Orleans, a group of Ursuline volunteers be sent instead. He knew of such a group, he advised the directors, and could make all the arrangements.

The Society of Jesus and the Order of St. Ursula had enjoyed a close relationship since the early days of the French Counter-Reformation. Chapters of the Ursulines often sprang up in the early 1600s in the wake of revival visits by itinerant Jesuits. The new women's order mirrored the Society of Jesus in its educational methods and missionary purposes, and Jesuit priests commonly served as the confessors and spiritual advisors for Ursuline nuns. In New France, the Ursulines supplied a pioneering female missionary campaign to match that of the Jesuits and continued to share the Jesuits' dedication to Indian conversion. For de Beaubois, a community of Ursuline nuns in New Orleans was tantamount to having Jesuit proxies there.

Marie Tranchepain, for her part, had long nursed a desire to follow in the footsteps of Marie of the Incarnation and join the ranks of foreign missionary Ursulines. When de Beaubois proposed the New Orleans plan to her, she saw it as perhaps her only chance to leave the convent in her native Rouen to advance the Ursuline ministry abroad. She had no difficulty recruiting a good-sized complement of like-minded Ursulines from other convents in the northwest of France. The Company of the Indies crafted a contract with this group of nuns that stipulated the hospital as their primary responsibility, making clear that teaching would be supplemental and could only be undertaken if it did not interfere with or detract from their nursing duties. Marie Tranchepain and the Ursulines who joined her understood that their physical passage to Louisiana was contingent on their agreement to add nursing to the scope of their mission and subordinate to it their educational ministry. However, their actions and the writing they have left us make it clear that it was their teaching apostolate that carried their souls across the Atlantic to New Orleans.

THE URSULINES IN FRENCH COLONIAL LOUISIANA

The Ursuline nuns who arrived in Louisiana in the summer of 1727 were hired to run a hospital but dreamed of converting Indians and of laying the foundation for an orthodox, observant Catholic community in the Lower Mississippi Valley by educating its young female French colonists.[14] Almost immediately,

14. This section on the Ursulines is based on Emily Clark, "A New World Community: The New Orleans Ursulines and Colonial Society, 1727–1803" (Ph.D. diss.,

the scope and nature of their mission took an unexpected turn. French colonial plans called for creating a plantation economy in Louisiana, and by the eighteenth century all Europeans in the Americas had uniformly embraced slave labor to achieve that end. Enslaved Africans and people of African descent made up more than a third of the population in the Lower Mississippi Valley on the eve of the nuns' arrival, and it was they, not Indians, who were destined to become the objects of the New Orleans Ursulines' missionary fervor.

The writings of the first generation of Ursulines give glimpses of this ministry's beginnings but offer us few clues about how the nuns regarded their work among the enslaved. There is no hint that the nuns disapproved of the institution. Indeed, they were themselves among the largest slaveowners in the colony.[15] On the other hand, they took the opposite stance of the planters of the Chesapeake and South Carolina, who opposed the conversion of the enslaved. They appear never to have doubted their course of action: within a few months they exchanged their vision of Indian conversion for a plan of African evangelization without a word of regret. The results of their work were significant. Over the course of the

---

Tulane University, 1998); Lierheimer, "Female Eloquence and Maternal Ministry"; Jane Frances Heaney, *A Century of Pioneering: A History of the Ursuline Nuns in New Orleans, 1727–1827,* ed. Mary Ethel Booker Siefken (New Orleans: Ursuline Sisters of New Orleans, Louisiana, 1993, written as Ph.D. diss., St. Louis University, 1949); and Rapley, *The Dévotes.*

15. The New Orleans Ursulines were atypical slaveholders in some respects. They insisted on sacramental marriage and kept couples and families together, which was unusual in colonial Louisiana, especially toward the end of the eighteenth century. And the nuns did not engage in staple crop agriculture, employing their slaves instead in dairying, vegetable gardening, housework, and skilled trades. See Clark, "A New World Community," chapter 3.

eighteenth century, people of African descent came to dominate the congregational ranks of the Catholic Church in New
Orleans. Toward the end of the colonial period and in the
early decades of the nineteenth century, free women of color
manifested both notable piety and leadership in the Church,
taking on themselves much of the work of evangelizing newly
enslaved Africans and slaves who came to New Orleans from
the Protestant areas of the young United States. In the 1830s a
group of pious free women of color banded together to form
a religious community that was eventually recognized as the
Sisters of the Holy Family.[16]

In the early eighteenth century, provincial Frenchwomen of
good breeding on the threshold of adulthood contemplated
quiet and respectable futures as wives of cultivated bourgeois
professionals. They would manage their households, raise their
children, go to church, and entertain their social peers in the
towns of their birth in modest but proper style. Some of them,
influenced by the nuns who educated them or by exceptionally
pious families, deviated from this mundane path to enter religious life in one of the convents in their hometowns. As a rule,
the well-born young women of eighteenth-century France, religious and lay, never really left home. The twelve Ursuline nuns
who came to New Orleans were, therefore, unusual, and the

16. For more about this evolution see Emily Clark and Virginia M. Gould,
"The Feminine Face of Afro-Catholicism in New Orleans, 1727–1852," *William and
Mary Quarterly,* 3d ser. 59, no. 2 (April 2002): 409–48. The relationship between the
Ursulines and slaves and issues of slavery and race relations are explored in depth in
Clark, "A New World Community," 120–58.

documents that follow should not be understood as representing a typical French colonial woman. The writings nonetheless provide us with new perspectives that broaden our understanding of early American life and womanhood. They reveal that the well-known Puritan women of New England had equally pious Catholic counterparts in Louisiana. We learn that, in contrast to the Anglican Church's ambivalence about evangelizing slaves in the British colonies, the Catholic Ursulines embraced the project of slave conversion with immediate enthusiasm. We find that decades before the flowering of Protestant female benevolence in the United States, nuns in New Orleans sheltered orphans and ran a hospital. And we discover that long before the education of women was made a priority by the young American republic, nuns made it their business to teach the female population of New Orleans, black and white alike. The documents that follow flesh out and complicate our portrait of early America. The teaching Ursulines of the eighteenth century would have been pleased to know that the things they wrote were destined to educate readers living nearly three hundred years after they first set foot in America.

PART I

LETTERS OF MARIE MADELEINE HACHARD

Lorient, France
February 22, 1727
My dear Father,

It was an honor for me to receive all the letters. You were so kind to write me. You asked me for an exact, detailed account of everything that happened on our way. It is your goodness that makes you take an interest in what concerns us. Therefore, we hasten to fulfill your wishes. Here is somewhat of a journal of our trip from Rouen to Lorient, the city by the sea at Brittany, near Port-Louis.[1]

1. Ordinarily, once a woman took her solemn vows as an Ursuline nun she was subject to the rule of cloister and did not leave the convent compound for any reason, even the death of a close relative. In medieval monasticism, the rule of cloister dictated that nuns neither ventured beyond the convent walls nor admitted any layperson, male or female, within the enclosure. The Ursulines observed a modified version of cloister that demanded that they remain within the convent but did allow female students to come and go to attend their schools. The Louisiana missionaries' travel overland in France and across the Atlantic was an exceptional event, for which the nuns received special permission from clerical authorities.

You know, my dear Father, that I believe that I have already had the honor of telling you that it is the Reverend Father de Beaubois of the Company of Jesus who formed the noble project of our establishment in New Orleans. This missionary is full of zeal and wisdom. You would not believe the number of obstacles he had to overcome to make this project succeed. He obtained everything with the help of God.

You also know, my dear Father, that our Reverend Mother Tranchepain, chosen to be superior; Mother Judde, chosen as the Assistant; and Mother Boulenger, chosen as treasurer, went ahead of us to Paris to make arrangements, in the name of our little community, with the gentlemen of the Company of the Indies.[2] These men, very zealous for religion, treated us with the greatest respect. The foundation seemed to us equally solid and advantageous.

After conducting our business in Paris concerning our establishment, our Reverend Mother Superior left for Hennebont with her two dear companions. It was important to undertake the necessary measures with the Reverend Father de Beaubois, the capable leader of this whole enterprise. The Reverend Father was at Hennebont, a city not far from Lorient, where he was awaiting the departure of a ship that sails regularly. Our Reverend Mothers had the joy of finding him there, but they could consult with him only for a few days, because Father had

2. Tranchepain, Judde, and Boulenger were among a total of twelve Ursulines who traveled to Louisiana in 1727. Eight of the missionary party were professed choir nuns: Tranchepain, Judde, Boulenger, Renée Yviguel of Vannes, Cécile Cavalier of Elboeuf, Marguerite Talaon of Ploermel, Jeanne Marion of Ploermel, and Madeleine Mahieu of Le Havre. Marie Madeleine Hachard was the only novice; Claude Massy the sole postulant. Two converse sisters, Marie-Anne Dain and Sister Anne, completed the party.

to sail, taking with him a good number of famous missionaries. I believe that they are now near Louisiana, the blessed country for which I long as if it were the Promised Land. I would like with all my heart, to be there in the monastery that has been built for us.[3]

About October 18, 1726, we received the order to go to Paris. The day of our departure was set for the twenty-fourth of the same month. If I seem to have left you, my dear Father, my dear Mother, and all my family without a tear and even with joy, my heart was not suffering any the less. I will confess that, at the last moment, I fought a hard battle within myself; but finally, the sacrifice was made, and I was pleased to have obeyed the Sovereign Master of our destiny. It is not necessary to retell all the acts of kindness from the Ursulines of Rouen, especially from Mesdames de Vigneral and de Lamberville, who are the heads of this kind and illustrious community. It is enough for me to assure you that I will never forget it.

Here our journal begins. If I cannot arouse your curiosity, I will at least have the merit of obeying you. Since you asked for details, I will try not to omit anything.

Thursday, October 24, 1726, I left Rouen by the Paris coach. I had as my companions two Ursuline religious who were to be a part of our community. One was Mother St. Francis Xavier, an Ursuline religious from Le Havre. The other was Mother Cavalier of Rouen, an Ursuline religious from Elboeuf. The two have very different temperaments; however, both were very kind. We had dinner at Fleury, and all of us went to spend

3. The monastery of which Hachard speaks existed at this time only in drawings. It was not completed until 1734.

the night at St. Clair. We arrived there very late. The roads were so bad that we had to travel on foot more than two leagues by night. I confess that I was very afraid to walk so long in the dark of night.

The next day, the twenty-fifth, we spent in Magny. At the request of the superior, the confessor of the Ursuline religious of this city detained us. We went up to the parlor to greet the superior, and we found there a well-prepared meal. We received from these ladies many acts of kindness.[4] They were very gracious. Our Mother Superior, Mother Tranchepain, and Mother Judde spent many years in this house, and they are held in great esteem. Doubtless, it was because of them that we were treated so well. We spent the night at Pontoise with the Ursulines of this city. We were well received there and treated very kindly.

On the twenty-sixth, we passed by St. Denis, and we arrived in Paris at four o'clock in the afternoon at the coach stop. There we found the extern of the Ursulines of Rue St. Jacques,[5] who had been waiting since nine o'clock in the morning with

4. Every Ursuline convent had a parlor, the only room in the monastery to which visitors were admitted. Only female students and nuns were permitted in other areas of the cloistered compound.

5. There were two types of nun in Ursuline convents. Choir nuns were fully professed religious sisters who took perpetual solemn vows. They were generally well educated, had bourgeois backgrounds, and entered the convent with a dowry. Choir nuns provided the instruction to students at Ursuline schools and controlled convent finances and leadership. Converse nuns were generally of humbler origins, often daughters of tradesmen, artisans, or laborers. They were less well educated and performed housekeeping and other support functions. Because converse nuns took simple vows, rather than perpetual solemn vows, they were not required to observe strict cloister. Consequently, one converse sister in each convent was designated the *touriere,* or extern sister, whose duty was to act as intermediary between the cloistered choir sisters and the world.

the order from the superior to rent a carriage for us. However, we had already contracted for a vehicle, which took us to the Ursulines of St. Jacques.[6] We were received very warmly there as well. They gave a room to each of us. The superior had the kindness to show us the way to the rooms herself.

We intended to remain only a very few days in Paris, but the Reverend Father d'Avangour, procurator of the Canadian Mission and of Louisiana, told us that we would be there more than one month. The boat had been designated for Lorient and our sailing vessel was not yet ready. It would be better to remain in Paris than in Lorient, where we would be bored. This delay distressed me. I thought day and night of our mission; however, I had to be patient. The kindness of all the Ursulines with whom I had the honor of staying eased my pain during our stay in Paris.

We were the recipients of countless acts of kindness. Mother St. Amand, the superior, a lady of infinite goodness, gave us books that we will need in our community. She offered to take care of arranging to send things from France to Louisiana when we needed them. I assure you, my dear Father, that we received from all these ladies the signs of the most sincere friendship. I

6. The Ursuline convent on the Rue St. Jacques on the Left Bank of Paris was among the oldest and most distinguished of more than three hundred Ursuline communities founded in France during the seventeenth century. In 1612 it also became the first Ursuline community to embrace the rule of cloister, or enclosure; Ursulines had not previously observed this practice. Each Ursuline community was independent, technically linked to others only by a shared mission and religious rule. The hospitality extended to the missionary party indicates, however, that Ursulines considered themselves bound to the members of their order regardless of community affiliation.

hesitate to tell you that in that earthly paradise, I was tempted, and this temptation was very real. But the Lord sustained me, and, fortified by His grace, I preferred to go to New Orleans instead of remaining in Paris. I will only confess to you that at the moment of separation there were tears on both sides. I felt that I was already attached and that without difficulty, I would have soon become accustomed to this kind house. However, my dear Father, when God speaks, we must obey. This should be a secret. I recognize that I am unworthy of the honor that these ladies wanted to confer on me by receiving me in their illustrious house.

It was uncertain after leaving Paris whether we would go by Orleans and then on the Loire to the place where we would embark, or whether we would go by way of Brittany. However, it was finally decided that we would travel by way of Brittany.

We departed from Paris with the Jesuits, Reverend Father Doutreleau and Brother Crucy, who were to come with us to Louisiana. On December 8, at five o'clock in the morning, after having attended Mass, we recited the prayer for travelers. Having eaten breakfast, we boarded the Brittany coach, which came to pick us up at the door of the convent. It cost forty livres for each person for the journey to Rennes, not counting the cost of food.[7] From Paris we went to dinner at Versailles. We were shown the magnificent palace of the King. There was ev-

---

7. The principal French unit of currency in the eighteenth century was the livre tournois. There were twenty sols to a livre and twelve deniers to a sol. Occasionally, money was counted in ecus, also known as crowns. There were three livres tournois to an ecu or crown. In 1727 there were approximately eleven British pence sterling to a French livre, so the coach fare would have been about 1.8 British pounds sterling.

erything there to satisfy curiosity, and I often had the thought of closing my eyes in order to mortify myself. This kind of mortification continues to challenge me.[8] In the evening we went to a village called La Queue. The next day, December 9, we had dinner at Dreux, a pretty, little, well-populated town. That evening we slept at Bresolles.

On the tenth we dined at Hodan. There we found a gentleman of good appearance who was traveling our way. He wanted to pay the coachman to take the eighth place in our coach, because he said that he wanted to pass the time more pleasantly in our good company. We were not comfortable with this situation. So, to discourage the man, Reverend Father Doutreleau explained that we had to keep silence for three hours in the morning and at night. The gentleman replied that if we did not wish to speak, he would pass the time talking with Brother Crucy. However, when he made himself known, we could see that we would need his assistance and that we should not treat him coldly. He was the chief official of Mayenne, where our luggage, that is, suitcases and packages, was to be inspected. He would be able to have us excused from the inspection, which always caused delay and embarrassment. We, therefore, accepted him, and he treated us most courteously.

Reverend Father Doutreleau asked him to use his influence in the city to prevent our luggage being opened. He promised to do so, and he kept his word. He had the kindness to go to the customs house, and nothing was inspected. We spent the night at Mortagne, after passing a very dangerous place where

8. Mortification consisted of various forms of self-denial and, in some cases, self-inflicted pain.

the coach from Caen to Paris had been robbed eight days earlier and the roads were becoming very bad. On the eleventh, we dined at Mesle, and we spent the night at Allençon. I cannot say anything about this city. We arrived there at night and departed the next day before daybreak. It was not yet three o'clock in the morning, and we were already on the road. The roads were so bad that hardly had we traveled half a league when we had to go on foot. Our coach became completely stuck in the mud. The drivers joined our twelve horses to twenty-two oxen in an effort to pull us out of this bad situation, which we had not expected.

We continued on our way and walked about one league. We were very cold, and since we did not find homes in which to rest on the way, we had to sit on the ground. The Reverend Father Doutreleau was on a little bluff near us. There, like John the Baptist, he exhorted us to do penance, and in the event we really needed to be patient. After resting a while, we continued on our way, and finally we had the good fortune of finding a little cottage where a poor woman was in bed. Only after much begging and promising did she open the door for us. She had neither wood nor candles. We had to make a fire with grass by whose light Reverend Father read his Breviary while waiting for the day. We did not fail to reward the charity of the good lady.

After more than ten hours, our carriage joined us. We could travel only forty-one leagues—almost entirely by walking. In spite of the fatigue, we laughed often. From time to time something amusing happened. We were all dirty up to our ears. The veils of our two Mothers were spotted with white dust. It was very amusing. We arrived at night at Mayenne, where the chief official wanted us to stay in his house. We did not think we should accept his offer, gracious though it was. We went to an inn, and we went to bed immediately because we were very tired. I forgot to tell you that when we were on the way, we did not keep six hours of perfect silence as previously announced by Reverend Father Doutreleau.

On the thirteenth we spent the night in Laval. It is a beautiful city. There is an Ursuline community, but we did not stay there that night because it was very late, and we did not want to inconvenience the community at that late hour. Besides, we were to leave the next day very early in the morning. It was Sunday. Father Doutreleau said Mass in the parish church across from the inn where we were staying. Later we drank a cup of chocolate for breakfast before departing. The whole city was at the door of our inn to see us board the coach. It was raining very hard, but this did not prevent the people from being on the street from five in the morning until eight, waiting for us. I noticed that the inhabitants of this city are as curious as the ones of Rouen.

We went to dinner at Vitrel. Brother Crucy was appointed to have food prepared for us at the inn while we went to greet the superior of the Ursulines of this city. She thought that Father Doutreleau was a priest of the Oratory. We let her believe that he was, and this mistake amused us very much. After an hour's conversation with the superior, we went by carriage to dine at the inn. All the people of the city were there to see us depart. Perhaps you will not believe that your daughter would one day incite the curiosity of entire cities.

This day, December fifteenth, we spent the night in a little village, where we found two Capuchin Fathers trying to find lodging at the inn.[9] Our Reverend Father invited them to have supper with us. We wanted to provide a good meal for them, but we could get only milk soup with an omelet and some little dessert. Even if we did not spend much, we laughed a great deal, for we were always in good humor.

Finally, on Tuesday the sixteenth, we arrived at Rennes, capital city of Brittany. The Ursulines were so kind as to send the extern a fourth of a league out to meet us. This good sister had us go into the house of one of the city's leading inhabitants to warm ourselves, for it was very cold. The master of the house received us kindly and brought us to a carriage that was waiting at the door to take us to the Ursulines.

I cannot tell you all the acts of kindness we received in this community. It was ten o'clock in the morning when we arrived, and we remained there until eight o'clock the next morning. During all this time, we received every possible act of kindness. Father Doutreleau stayed at the Jesuit house.

Several Reverend Fathers of this college honored us with a visit to the parlor and invited us to visit their house and their church. The college of Rennes is a thousand times more beautiful than the one of Rouen. The buildings are magnificent and comfortable. Although the church is very beautiful, I find the church of Rouen more striking. I also prefer the garden of the college of our city. While visiting the college, we received many

9. It is evident from this passage that Hachard wrote this letter in stages.

acts of kindness from the Fathers. Meanwhile, Brother Crucy was busy putting in good order the two conveyances that he had procured for us to continue on our way. He came to take us to the coach office. The price of these coaches was twenty livres each for taking us on a one-day trip from Rennes to Hennebont. We went to dinner at Hors and spent the night at Hennebont. Father Doutreleau sent his valet on horseback to announce our arrival to Mother Tranchepain, our dear Louisiana Superior. She had been living for some time with the Ursulines of Hennebont where she was waiting for us. Since it was late, this wise Mother told us to spend the night in the inn, in order not to disturb the community that was not her own. She said she would send an extern the next day to conduct us to the monastery. We easily obeyed these reasonable orders.

The next morning we arrived at the Ursuline monastery and our dear Superior received us with open arms and treated us with great kindness. The superior of the house, a lady of much goodness, welcomed us with the same warmth. She gave an outside room to Father Doutreleau. One day after our arrival, two Ursuline religious of Ploermel arrived, accompanied by the Reverend Father Tartarin, a missionary Jesuit destined for Louisiana. We also have one religious from Hennebont; thus our community is composed of eight professed religious. Mother Tranchepain, superior; Mesdames Judde and Boulenger of the house of Rouen; Mother St. Francis Xavier from the house of LeHavre; Mother Cavalier of the house of Elboeuf; two ladies of the house of Ploermel; and one of the house of Hennebont. There are two postulants: Sister le Massy, who comes from Tours, and I, and one converse sister,

Sister Françoise. We are eleven women in all, without counting two servants. There are many communities in France that are not as numerous, and I doubt very much that there are many where the members are as united and more content with their life.[10]

I forgot to tell you, my dear Father, that all along the way from Paris to Hennebont we were almost always at war— Brother Crucy and I. Reverend Father D'Avangour appointed me to be Brother's directress and Madame St. Amand, Superior of St. Jacques, asked him to be my director. We fulfilled our appointments beautifully; from time to time we told some truths frankly to each other. Everything was done in a playful way. I am not melancholic by nature; the good brother is not either. From time to time we laughed at ourselves, but since we were the youngest, we were naturally the subject of conversation.

Fathers Tartarin and Doutreleau, who were to make the trip with us, left the next day for Lorient to see about the ship that was to take us to Louisiana. We saw them off at the door of the monastery by the sea. The two priests got in a nice little boat, and we wished them a good trip.

Before leaving Rouen, our Reverend Mothers granted me two favors: first, to begin my novitiate the day of my departure from Rouen to Paris; and, second, to be permitted to take the holy habit at Hennebont. After receiving my bap-

---

10. The nuns from Ploermel were Marguerite Talaon, known as Sister St. Thérèse, and Jeanne Marion, known as Sister St. Michel. Hachard misidentifies the origin of Renée Yviguel, known as Sister St. Marie, who was from Vannes, not Hennebont. She also fails to mention a twelfth sister who was known to have made the voyage to Louisiana, Marie-Anne Dain, a converse sister.

tismal certificate, which you were so kind to have sent me, I reminded Mother Tranchepain of her promise. She listened to me kindly and kept her promises faithfully. Reverend Father Doutreleau was so kind as to go to Vannes to ask permission from the Bishop, who gave it without difficulty. My clothing ceremony took place on the nineteenth of January 1727, with much solemnity. I took the name of St. Stanislaus. Mother Tranchepain, our Superior, entertained the entire community of Hennebont. The day after my clothing, they gave me a black veil that I would keep during all the trip.[11] (See fig. 1.)

From Hennebont, we sailed in a boat in which Monsieur Morin, a rich merchant from Lorient, had kindly come with our Reverend Fathers to pick us up and bring us to Lorient. We were very comfortable during the sea trip, which lasted two leagues. We stayed at the home of Monsieur Morin. He is

11. Entry into the Ursuline order occurred only after two preliminary stages were completed. The first stage was postulancy, a period lasting anywhere from several months to a year or more. During this time, a young woman lived at the convent according to the rule of the Order but wore ordinary, modest dress augmented with a simple, short headscarf that partially covered her hair. The purpose of the postulancy was to determine the young woman's suitability for convent life. Eventually, if she was judged a promising candidate and if she still wished to pursue a religious life, she was admitted to the novitiate. The novitiate was a more formal status that entailed submission to the convent superior and chapter, and observation of all elements of the Order's rule. A young woman's formal status as a novice was recognized in the clothing ceremony, a service conducted by a priest, at which the new novice received the habit of the Order to wear. She was given a long white veil that completely covered her hair. A celebration often followed the clothing ceremony. After satisfactorily completing a novitiate of two to three years, the young woman took her final solemn vows of profession, at which point the white veil was exchanged for the black veil of the fully professed choir nun. By giving Marie Hachard a black veil to put away in anticipation of her taking her final vows, the Louisiana missionaries signaled their confidence in her suitability for religious life and the missionary venture that she had joined.

a very polite gentleman, and we owe him a great deal. In his home we were almost as comfortable as in a convent. We had there a room that we used as choir; another room served as refectory; and several other rooms as dormitories.

On our voyage, our Reverend Fathers took a carpenter, a locksmith, and several other workers with them. As for us, my dear Father, do not be scandalized, for it is the manner of the country, we took a Moor to serve us.[12] We also took a pretty little cat that wanted to be a part of our community, taking for granted that he could find little mice and rats in Louisiana just as in France.

I am not angry about the talk that goes on in Rouen about me. Some people say that I have not left and that they see me often. It is marvelous for me to be seen at the same time in two cities so far from each other. I recall having read in the life of St. Francis Xavier that this great apostle of the Indies and of Japan was often in several places at the same time. This is considered a great miracle. I am not, dear Father, a saint big enough to work miracles. I am certainly not in Rouen, but in Lorient, and I am always very happy and joyful in my vocation. I intend to fulfill my duties as well as possible.

On the second of this month, two missionary Jesuits departed from here on a boat for Pontichery. Before their departure, they honored us by coming to see us and dining with us

12. To describe the enslaved servant who traveled with the nuns, Marie Hachard uses the word *Morre,* a word that was not commonly used to describe enslaved Africans. In Louisiana, enslaved men and women were called *nègres* and *nègresses,* respectively, and Marie changed to this usage once she arrived in the colony, suggesting that her use of the word *Morre* in this passage reflects her inexperience with the terminology of slavery rather than the geographic origin or religious belief of the individual to whom she refers.

several times. They wanted to convince half of our community to found a convent of Ursulines at Pontichery, but Reverend Father Tartarin did not want to let any of us go. We have the consolation of being transported to Louisiana on a boat where all the important officers appear to be honest men.

Our Reverend Fathers do not want us to say "Ours," as we do in the convent, when speaking of anything we use. They say that the first thing we would hear is the sailors making fun of our way of speaking and saying "our soup," "our bonnet," and so forth. I will confess that I cannot prevent myself from using the forbidden word, and I even say "our nose!" Father Tartarin often tells me: "My Sister, raise 'our head.'" This makes us laugh and diverts us from fatigue. Reverend Father Tartarin warned us that he will make fun of us if we get seasick on the voyage, especially of the first one getting sick. I wish to be the first, because once I get over it, it will be my turn to laugh at the others.

We loaded a number of lambs in our boat, and 500 chickens will travel with us. As you see, no one wants to die of hunger on the way.

Finally, my dear Father, the day came, the day so desired, of our departure. The wind was favorable, and they announced to us that we would sail in an hour. I cannot tell you the joy of all our community. My joy would be without equal if it were not for the pain of being away from you and from my dear mother, who has done so much for me; and for this I will be grateful to her all my life. When I think of all the acts of kindness you have done for me, I cannot help being touched. I hear only the voice of God, and I follow it as the only One

Who can separate me from my dear parents, whom I embrace with all my heart.

Now we are going to sail, even though the packages of Mother Cavalier and mine, which had been sent here via Le-Havre to be transported, might not yet have arrived. Perhaps God judged them superfluous and has permitted them to fall to the bottom of the sea. May God's holy will be done. If they arrive here, they will be sent to us on another boat. Monsieur Morin has the kindness to come with a great number of important inhabitants of the city to take us up to three leagues on the sea, and they will come back this evening in a boat.

I wonder how we are going to be able to climb up to our boat since it is so high. Reverend Father Tartarin says that he will put us two by two in a bag, and someone will lift us with a pulley as they do for cargo. But our captain, though inexperienced with this kind of merchandise, assures us that he will see that we are taken comfortably seated, one after the other.

Goodbye, my very dear Father, I beg you to let me hear from you. I have nothing in the world dearer than you and my dear mother. Nothing less than the glory of God and the needs of the poor inhabitants could have made me leave you. I assure you that I will be separated from you only in body. I will be with you in spirit and in heart, but since I cannot do anything by myself, I turn to the One Who can fill you with blessings. I pray every day for your health and the sanctification of your soul. I ask you not to forget me. All my life I will have a profound respect and profound gratitude for you.
My very dear Father,

Your most humble and most obedient daughter and servant
Hachard of St. Stanislaus.

New Orleans
October 27, 1727
My dear Father,

   I had the honor of receiving your letter dated last April 6,
which I received the twentieth of this month, eve of the feast
of St. Ursula, as I was coming out of retreat. Just imagine, my
dear Father, my joy at hearing news of you, of my dear mother,
and of my sisters. You should have received by now two of my
letters; one, written the day before our departure from Lorient,
city in lower Brittany, and the other from the Caille St. Louis,
one of the ports of the island of Saint Domingue. In the first
letter, dated the twenty-second of February 1727, I told you all
that happened on our way from Rouen up to our sailing; and in
the second, dated May 14, I wrote of our arrival on this island.[13]
You see, my dear Father, that I do not miss any opportunity to
let you know of my perfect gratitude for all your kindness to
me, especially for your consent to my departure against the advice of so many persons who opposed God's designs. Of all the
things for which I am obliged to you, I see this last instance as
the greatest and the most pleasing to God. Since my gratitude,
as perfect as it might be, is such a small thing, I call on Our
Lord every day and pray that He be your reward and keep you
in perfect health.

   13. The letter that Hachard refers to as being written in Saint Domingue the
previous May was either lost or was not printed for some other reason. She supplies
the details of the transatlantic crossing in a separate missive that she enclosed with
this letter.

Those who told you that we were in great danger during the fifteen days at the anchorage of Lorient are certainly mistaken. It is true that we had about one hour of danger, but after that, we shook our ears like school children and went on our way. Nothing more happened except that a little water got into our boat. We had to pump out the water every two hours and sometimes more often. It could have been that the inhabitants of Lorient believed that we were lost, but even if that had been true, we would have been lost by the Grace of God, and only to the world. But no, Our Lord was not content with our good will only. He wants to see the effects of it.

You tell me that my sister, Louison, is a postulant at Val-de Grace. I wish with all my heart that she will become a religious in this holy house. She will have the advantage of living there with a person whose virtue and merit I greatly admire. That is, Mother de Quevreville. Our Lord gave her, like me, a vocation for joining the establishment in Louisiana. I counted on making the trip in such wonderful company, but family reasons detained her in France. If my sister believes me, she will follow exactly the advice of Reverend Father de Houppeville, my former director, and now her director. I want him to be as helpful to her as he was to me.

I will be very happy if my sister, Elizabeth, continues her stay at St. Francis. What happiness for her if she could be a religious there with my oldest sister. I am sure that you will let me know about the progress my brother is making in sciences. The most ardent desire of my heart is that one day he be either a good holy priest or a fervent Jesuit missionary. The brother of one of our Mothers is a missionary some five or six hundred leagues from here, the Reverend Father Boulenger, Jesuit. I am, however, a little angry with my brother because he has not written to me at all. If he does not have a pen, he can tell me with confidence, and I will send him one, or if it is because he has forgotten how to write, it is another thing, and I beg him to relearn and to give me his news at the first opportunity. I await the same favor from my sister, Dorothy, whom I embrace with all my heart.

My brother, the religious, has not done me the honor of writing to me. Would it be that he is angry with me or that he thinks that I am angry with him? It is true that to deter me from my plan he told me before my departure many things that could not make me pleased. But I regard all of that as a test and even as proof of his affection. My dear Father, when one is certain of doing God's will, one values as nothing the opinions of men. Many people considered our enterprise as folly, but what is folly in the eyes of the world is wisdom in the eyes of the Lord. If my dear brother is still angry with me because I did not defer blindly to his advice, I beg you to make peace for me. If I do not write him, it is because being naturally timid, I dare not take this liberty without his permission. I believe, however, that he has not forgotten me during our voyage. I even believe that I felt the effect of his prayers several times when, I assure you, we might have perished. Everyone in our boat, the *Gironde*, said that out of ten boats having the same trouble, as ours, not one could escape.[14] It must have been that good souls were praying for us. At the head of these good souls I would al-

14. Hachard may be referring to the threats from pirates she mentions on pages 48, 53, and 58–59 and the instances when the *Gironde* struck rocks or ran aground, which she describes on pages 48 and 59–63.

ways put my dear brother. I beg you to assure him that I retain for him always the most sincere affection.

Although I do not know yet know the country of Louisiana perfectly, I am nonetheless, my dear Father, going to give a little detail. I can assure that it does not seem that I am at the Mississippi. There is here as much beauty and politeness as in France. Gold and velvet cloth is very common, although three times more expensive than in Rouen. Bread costs ten sols a pound; it is made with flour from India or from Turkey. Eggs cost forty-five or fifty sols a dozen. Milk is fourteen sols per pot, which holds half the amount in France.[15] We eat meat, fish, peas, wild beans, several kinds of vegetables and fruits such as pineapple, which is the best of all the fruits, watermelons, potatoes, Sabotines, which are more or less like apples of the grade Rainette in France, figs, pecans, cashew nuts, which, as soon as you eat them stick in the throat, Girmons, which are like a kind of pumpkin, and many other fruits that I do not know yet.

Finally, we live off the meat of wild beef, goats, geese, and wild turkeys, rabbits, chicken, ducks, pheasants, partridges, quail, and other fowl, and game of different kinds. The rivers are full of monstrous fish, especially catfish, which is an excellent fish; rays; carp; salmon and an infinity of other fishes that are unknown in France. One makes much use here of chocolate with milk and of coffee. A lady here has given us a good supply

15. A French sol was worth slightly more than half a British pence sterling in 1727, which meant that a dozen eggs would cost well over a shilling, a considerable sum. If a family were to make up a weekly shopping cart of Hachard's list, the annual total would have come to over nine British pounds sterling in 1727, a sum that was not likely within reach of the average inhabitant of colonial Louisiana.

and we take some every day. Three days a week in Lent we eat meat, and the rest of the year we eat meat on Saturday, as on the Island of Saint Domingue. We accustom ourselves readily to the wild food of this land. We eat bread that is half rice and half flour. There are wild grapes, bigger than the French grapes, but they are not in a bunch. They serve them on a plate similar to plums. What one eats more, and which is more common, is rice with milk and some sagamité, which one makes with Indian flour ground with a mortar. Then the flour is boiled in water with butter or some kind of grease. The people of all of Louisiana find this food very good.

I have been curious to know the state of the land of this country, in order, my dear father, to be able to give you some little idea. You refer to this place here sometimes as Louisiana and sometimes as Mississippi, but it should be Louisiana. This is the name given to the country by Monsieur Robert Cavelier, Sieur de LaSalle, native of Rouen, when he came with Monsieur Joustel and several other persons of the same city to make the first discoveries in 1676 and 1685.[16] In honor of the reign of Louis the Great, the name Louisiana has remained. But the name Mississippi is for the river that is called thus, to which the said Sieur de LaSalle gave the name Colbert River, because Monsieur Colbert was then Minister of State. But the name of Colbert did not remain, and one continued to call it the Mississippi River. At present, several people call it the St. Louis River. It is the largest river in all America, with the exception of the St. Lawrence. An infinite number of tributaries join the

16. The French honorific *sieur* is roughly equivalent to *sir* in English.

Mississippi. There are seven to eight hundred leagues from the source to the Gulf of Mexico, into which it empties. It is not navigable, however, by large ships, but only by small sloops that can carry twelve to fifteen persons. Inasmuch as this river is boarded by forests of high trees, the swiftness of the waters erodes the river bank such that the trees there fall, and a quantity of them come together at certain points and block the flow of the river. It would be a great expense and a great deal of work if one wanted to clear all the trees to make the river navigable and in a condition to allow ships to travel up and down stream. Moreover, there are many sandbanks, and it would be necessary to build an embankment.

We are nearer to the sun here than in Rouen, without, however, having very great heat. The winter is very moderate. It lasts about three months, but there is but a little light frost. They assure us that Louisiana is four times larger than France. The land is very fertile and brings several harvests each year, but not along the river and the tributaries, for there it is for the most part forests of oaks and other trees of prodigious height and girth and reeds and cane that grow from ten, fifteen, and twenty feet in height. But some leagues away there are prairies, plains, and fields where grow a quantity of trees called cottonwood, which produce no cotton, sycamores, berry bushes, chestnuts, figs, almonds, walnuts, lemons and oranges, pomegranates, and other trees which make the country beautiful. If the land were cultivated, there would be none better in the world. However, to accomplish that, it would be necessary to be populated differently, bringing from France workers of all skills. A man working the ground for only two days and sow-ing wheat could harvest more than enough to feed himself the whole year. But most of the people here live in idleness and occupy themselves mostly with hunting and fishing. The Company conducts much commerce in the fur trade, beavers and other merchandise, with the savages, who are very sociable people for the most part. That is all that I can tell you of the state of the country. I shall inform you more fully later, when I shall have learned more.

You have advised me, dear Father, that you have bought two large maps of the state of Mississippi, and that you do not find New Orleans there. It must be that these maps are old, because one would not have omitted this capital city of the country. I am sorry that you spent 110 sols and were not able to find the location of our residence. I believe that they will make new maps where our establishment will be shown.

We made an eight-day retreat before St. Ursula's Day. Reverend Father de Beaubois gave three talks a day. Our young postulant from Tours took the habit on St. Ursula's Day, and my sister, Françoise, is going to take it on All Saints' Day. We are as well lodged here as one could wish, awaiting the completion of our convent's construction. There is not another religious house that has been so well off at its start. Upon arriving here, Reverend Father de Beaubois told us that he just lost nine blacks who had perished in a single storm of north wind. This is a loss of nine thousand livres. The Company of the Indies gave us eight of them two weeks ago, of whom two then fled, apparently into the woods or elsewhere. Fourteen or fifteen of the Company's fled the same day. We kept a handsome woman to serve us, and the rest we sent to our habitation to cultivate our land.[17] This place is but a league from here. We have a manager and his wife who are charged to tend our interests there.

We observe cloister here with as much regularity as the convents of France. If we had the misfortune of Reverend Father de Beaubois getting sick and being unable to come to say Mass, we would be without it on Easter Day and even for six months, rather than go out of our convent to attend Mass at the parish church.

The Reverend Fathers Tartarin and Doutreleau departed six weeks ago to establish their posts near the Illinois tribe. Our Reverend Father Superior is now alone here with Brother Parisel.

I will not speak to you at all, my dear Father, of the morals of the secular people of this country. I do not know them and have no wish at all to know them, but it is said that their morals are quite corrupt and quite scandalous. There is also a

17. Charles R. Maduell Jr., comp. and trans., *The Census Tables for the French Colony of Louisiana from 1699 through 1732* (Baltimore: Genealogical Publishing, 1972), 127. Neither the Ursulines nor the Jesuits were actually given slaves. The demand for slaves always exceeded the supply in Louisiana. The proprietors of Louisiana, the Company of the Indies, sold the Ursulines and the Jesuits slaves from its holdings. This was understood as a favor in the context of the competition among inhabitants to purchase slaves. It is unfortunately impossible to determine from surviving records what became of the "handsome woman" Hachard mentions, but we know from the censuses of 1731 and 1732 that there were sixteen adults and three children on the nuns' plantation, and none living in town with the nuns as domestic servants. Whether the increase from eight to nineteen slaves occurred through purchase or natural increase is impossible to determine from existing records.

The French colonial habitation was the equivalent of the British colonial plantation or farm. It was not always planted with cash crops such as sugarcane, tobacco, rice, or indigo. The Ursulines, for example, used their land to supply them with food, including dairy products.

large number of honest people. One cannot see at all any of the girls that were said to have been sent here by force. None seem to have come this far. You say, my dear Father, that the Reverend Father de Houppeville makes all his dévotes into nuns.[18] We need this Reverend Father here, not to make nuns, but to make dévotes, because a Capuchin Father assured us the other day that there is not even one in all the country, nor in the surrounding area.

All our Mothers are in perfect health, except our Reverend Mother Superior, whom we have had the sadness to see nearly always sick since we arrived. She is, however, a little better than she was. She sends you greetings, as does all our Community.

I assure you, my dear Father, that the Sisters in the Community have shown much kindness to me, especially our loving Mother Superior. The longer I am under her direction, the more I love her. I receive new signs of tenderness every day. What troubles me is that I do not deserve this. I could not be happier, as much as one can be in this world. And who would not be happy in the company of holy sisters? One can easily see that it was the good God Who has chosen His subjects, for there is not one of our Mothers who does not have infinite merit and the most perfect devotion, especially our Reverend Mother Superior, and Mother St. Francis Xavier, the Mistress of Novices, who was with the Ursulines of LeHavre and with whom I departed from Rouen. We would not be surprised

18. A dévot (male) or dévote (female) was a French layperson who seriously pursued a pious life. They customarily submitted themselves to a clerical spiritual director who regularly heard their confession and guided their spiritual progress. Such spiritual directors often influenced dévots' decisions to enter religious life.

to see them perform miracles. It is up to me to walk in their footsteps, to follow their example, and to imitate them in everything I can.

I suppose that my oldest sister is in good health. I am surprised that she has not written to me. I embrace her with all my heart, and I recommend myself to her holy prayers.

I forgot to tell you, my dear Father, that while we were in danger on the *Gironde,* I promised six Masses to the souls in purgatory, on condition that you would have the goodness to have them said, being persuaded of your good heart, and that you will not refuse me.

This package will travel on the *Prince de Conty* which just brought us some blacks from Guinea. The *Gironde* departs from here at the same time, as does the *Dromadaire,* but I hope that the *Prince de Conty* is the best boat and will arrive first in France and will deposit at that instant this package at the post office of Lorient to be held for you.

I assure you, my dear father, that distance does not diminish the esteem and the respect I have always had for you. If I were not as content in my vocation as I am, the distance from you would be a great sadness for me.

I am perfectly well, by the grace of the Lord. I hope that your health is as good. I was not seasick at all, though our crossing was very long and very difficult because the winds were nearly always contrary. I am sending you an account of our entire voyage. It will please you, I am sure. I close for now, fearing I bore you. Good-bye, my very dear father. I embrace you a thousand times. But, no, I cannot because you are too far. Therefore, I ask my dear brother to perform this amiable commission for me. I am, with all my heart, in profound respect and in perfect gratitude.

My dear Father,

Your very humble and obedient daughter and servant.

Hachard of St. Stanislaus

New Orleans

October 27, 1727[19]

You expressed the wish, dear Father, that I would give you an account of our trip. It is because of your good heart that you take an interest in all that concerns us. I am so grateful, that I do what you wish. Here is a general account of all that happened since I left France. As you see, I am very faithful in giving you this account.

We sailed February 22, 1727, on the *Gironde,* under the command of Monsieur Vauberci. The second in command was Monsieur Gueret, who was so kind to us that we will never forget all he did for us. Before sailing, we went to say good-bye to Monsieur Dusaillet, Commander of Lorient and Director of the Company of the Indies. We are also grateful to him. From there we went to the boat with Monsieur and Madam Morin and many other friends who wanted to be with us at our departure. The two Captains received us on board, but the wind changed, and it was decided to postpone our departure until the next day. This delay gave us time to get settled in our rooms.

19. In the version of the letters published in Rouen in 1728, this letter is placed out of chronological sequence, following a letter bearing the same date but relating subsequent events.

A partition had been erected for us between decks—eighteen feet long and seven feet wide. We were together in this place, six beds on each side, three bunks, one over the other, in a way that we could not sit on our beds without touching the floor. I can assure you that I was often trapped since I was one of those who had the upper bunk to which they had assigned the lightest persons. One of our Sisters, the thirteenth, had to sleep below, in the passageway.[20]

In this place, we had only two portholes for a window, the size of two hands, but very often we could not open them because the water would come to spray onto the beds. We had to get up and lie down again, one after another. We could not be in our room more than two or three at the same time. In spite of the extreme heat that we endured in this oven, the Lord always kept us in perfect health, and we had the consolation of being alone in our room. All the other passengers were together in the St. Barbe area.[21] Our Reverend Fathers fared worse than we did. They had only a small little hole that did not admit any daylight. They could not stay there because of the excessive heat. They decided to sleep on the open deck. Exposed to the wind and the rain they covered their heads with laundry baskets to protect their heads from the rain.

We set out the next day, February 23, at two o'clock in the afternoon. The weather was good. We were in good com-

20. This is the only reference to a thirteenth sister. It is possible that a combination of thirteen choir and converse Ursulines made the transatlantic voyage, but only twelve are mentioned by name in the historical record. Hachard may have included Miss Delachaise in her count, as she notes that this young woman was lodged on the ship in the nuns' quarters.

21. The St. Barbe was the gun room.

pany on the deck when a half league from Lorient, our boat twice struck a rock. The shock of the impact was very great and caused alarm on the vessel as they hoisted the sail. At the port of Lorient, they noticed the problem and informed Monsieur Dusaillet that the boat was stranded. The gentleman and several other persons came to our aid. He told us that it was said that we had an accident in the port. He reassured us that there was nothing to fear and that many people were vigorously working on the problems. We were freed from this first scare and ready to continue our voyage. Our vessel did not sustain any damage at all from this terrible blow. It was at this time that the people began to pay tribute to the sea. No one escaped seasickness, but those who were less sick, Mother Boulenger and I, had only stomach distress.

The winds changed and became very contrary. The boat was in constant agitation and leaped in such a way that we were thrown on one another. As soon as the soup was poured, it spilled on to the tablecloth, unless one held it with two hands, as only a sailor can do because the rest of us had enough to do to hold ourselves up. That contributed sometimes to our laughter. As for seasickness, which is a very violent sickness that reduces people to feeling near death, once we knew what it was, we realized that it would not kill us. Our Reverend Mother Superior was the one who was sick the longest, but that did not diminish her zeal and her profound courage for the glory of God. It was enough for us to look at her to be encouraged not only to suffer with patience but with joy. We had the consolation of seeing that in spite of seasickness, the other trials that were caused by the storms, the length of the trip, and the

encounter with Corsaires, no one of us regretted our own sacrifice for God or even appeared to be worrying about the risks
involved with the bad weather.[22]

It was in this situation that our Reverend Mother Superior
made a plea in her name and in that of the Community to the
Blessed Mother and St. Francis Xavier, imploring their protection. The storm raged so strongly and the sea was so violent
that it caused the death of forty-nine sheep and a number of
chickens that had been loaded onto our ship for food. They
were found suffocated and were thrown into the sea. That diminished our food supply considerably and we had to eat rice
with water, and salted beef, but some bacon was so bad that we
could not eat it. Not having butter, our beans were prepared
with lard. But this bad food did not damage our health. In
addition, because the wind was against us, the vessel advanced
hardly at all. In fifteen days we progressed only as far as we
normally would have in three days. That also diminished our
water supply. We and all other persons on board were reduced
to one-half pint of water a day. Moreover, the water was very
bad. If the captains had had favorable winds, they would have
stopped at the Canary Islands to get some water; however, the
winds favored only the return to Port Louis, which obliged our
Captain to stop at the Island of Madeira, March 12, about three
hundred leagues from Lorient.

This island belongs to the King of Portugal. It is divided
into three cities. The principal one is Episcopalle, and it was

22. *Corsaire* was the term applied to the privateers or pirates who menaced ships
off the west coast of Africa.

there that we stopped. As soon as they saw us, they sent a canoe to find out what we wanted. The persons sent were satisfied with our answers. The Captain greeted the city with seven cannon shots. The city answered him with five cannon shots. We anchored there immediately thereafter. Those who came to see us reported that on our vessel there was a convent of religious and several missionary Jesuits. This news incited their curiosity and drew many visitors to us. The Fathers of the Company of Jesus, who had a famous college in this city, were the first to come on board to see us. They did not give our Fathers any time to prepare for their arrival.

No one could have been more gracious than the Fathers were. There was only one who spoke French, and he told us many nice things in the name of all of them. They insisted that we land and take lodging in their house. We thanked them but we declined. Our Reverend Fathers went the next morning to dine with them. They were received with great politeness and were treated magnificently. They were given a ram as a present.

We also shared in the generosity of the Madeira Fathers. They themselves brought us big baskets filled with all kinds of refreshments, such as lemons in abundance, lettuce, preserves, and many other things. During the three days that we remained in this place, these generous and gracious Fathers visited with us several times and appeared to take great pleasure in seeing us, praising our considerable zeal that made us undertake this long and difficult journey. The greatest pain for them was that they did not think that they could do enough for us. They were feeling that what they did for us was nothing in comparison with how much they wanted to do. Several

Fathers there had thick glasses on their noses, as is the fashion
in Portugal. I noticed a young one who took them off to read
something. This seems to me very extraordinary. Their ways of
acting are more or less similar to those of our Fathers in France,
except that they wear their hair shorter.

We saw many other important gentlemen of the city,
among them the Superintendent of the City. All were dressed
in black. Each one wore a reliquary and a rosary on his neck.
The Inquisition was in this city, as it is in Portugal and Spain.
The Jesuit students were also curious and came to see us. We
were delighted. They all carried a rosary in their hands that
give them an aura of importance, but they say that they are not
any more devout than other people. Our Reverend Fathers find
the church of the Jesuits magnificent. The front of the altar is
made of massive silver, and the walls are porcelain. There is no
church in France as rich in ornaments as this one. The trees on
this island were heavy with ripe fruit in the month of March.
We did not see any women. They are not visible. One sees them
through grills. They go out only to attend Mass, and all of them
at the same time, so that they form a kind of procession. They
walk covered with big veils and in silence unless they are saying
the rosary.

There are two convents on this island. The more important
one is of the Order of St. Claire. The Abbess is a Portuguese
Princess. As they are freer than the secular people, the talk of
our arrival soon reached them. The Abbess wrote a very gracious letter to our Reverend Mother Superior to invite her and
all the community to her home. She praised us very much. Her
style was genteel, at least that is the way the officer explained it

to us. The letter was written in Portuguese, and our Reverend Mother answered it in French. The Abbess received the letter of our loving Mother with great expressions of esteem and friendship, although she did not understand anything, unless it was translated for her by someone who knew French and Portuguese. The next day, a young lady from the boat went to visit her in the name of our Community. She was overwhelmingly showered with kind words and presents. The religious of this monastery, who numbered more than 300, embraced her at the door of the convent reiterating their invitation to us to their home. Having the water we needed, we made the decision not to accept the invitation, and we also wished to edify the public by remaining attached to the cloister of the *Gironde* rather than appear in a city where even the laywomen do not show themselves. Finally, we thanked the city by firing a cannon shot, and we continued on our way. I believe that if we had remained anchored a longer time, the religious, less attached to the cloister than we, would have left the convent to come to see us. They have heard of our modesty and the modesty of our habit, which they found very different from theirs. They were impressed, as were the Reverend Jesuit Fathers.[23]

23. It is unlikely that the Portuguese Clarists would have left their convent to visit the Ursulines aboard the *Gironde*. The Clarist Order practiced a stricter form of cloister than the Ursulines with respect to observance of enclosure and restrictions on visitors. The young laywoman who was sent to the Clarist convent to bear greetings from the shipboard nuns was, for instance, met at the entrance of the convent and not admitted within. However, within their convent walls Iberian nuns led a life that sometimes approached the luxurious, with richly furnished private living quarters, personal servants, and fine clothing that often strayed far from the monastic severity exemplified by the French Ursulines' black serge habits.

The wind was favorable for only two days, and then it changed against us so that it took us a long time to advance 200 leagues, at the end of which we discovered a Corsair ship. At least we thought so by its appearance. Immediately we began to make preparations necessary for combat. Each one armed himself. The cannons were charged, and everybody took his post. It was decided that during combat we would remain locked up between decks. The laywomen dressed as men. There were only three, and it was done only to increase the number of the crew; however, they said good-bye to their husbands. Mademoiselle Delachaise—who was always with us—cried bitterly for fear of losing her brother in combat. He was an ensign and his post was on the bridge. The first captain was on deck, and Father Tartarin was with him. The place of the second captain was on the forecastle. Father Doutreleau was with him. Brother Crucy was on the bridge to provide ammunition to all these fighters who were armed up to the teeth and filled with admirable courage. We were armed with only the rosary in our hands. We were not sad, thanks to God. Nobody in our company showed any weakness. We were charmed to see the courage of our officers and passengers, who looked as if they were going to beat the enemy at the first blow. All these preparations were unnecessary. The enemy vessel, after having circled around us several times, seeing us in a state of defense, and feeling less strong, left us in peace.

But it was a sad freedom for religious to be on a boat where it was impossible to have a moment to one's self. We took the time for our spiritual exercises, but it was in the midst of dissipation that always exists among people who think of passing their time only in amusements. This is what caused our greatest grief.

On Good Friday we finally arrived on the Tropic, that is to say on the line of the sun.[24] The sanctity of the day prevented us from celebrating the baptismal ceremony of which you have doubtlessly heard. It was postponed until Saturday after dinner. I will not give you the details of this ceremony, which is not only an amusement for the sailors but so much more because one has to pay money to be exempt from participating in it. We were more than twenty in our company, including the servants and the Reverend Fathers as well as the others. They gained more than two pistoles from us.[25] Those of the passengers who did not want to pay anything were doused with several buckets of water on their bodies, but the tremendous heat made this bath agreeable.

Several days later, we had a second alarm with the encounter of a similar enemy vessel, which pursued us very closely. We prepared our defense, and when we saw it very near, we locked ourselves in the place assigned to us. We were ready to fire upon the enemy, but he retreated. That reassured us for a few hours and gave us time for supper. As we noticed that it was nearing, and retreating, from time to time, we were on alert all night. We went to bed expecting that we could be awakened at any moment, but this did not come to pass, as the enemy ship finally left us.

If we had any consolation, it was the opportunity to par-

24. The equator.
25. A *pistole* was a gold Spanish coin worth about four livres tournois.

ticipate in the Holy Sacrifice of the Mass. It was celebrated every day, and very often we had the blessing of fortifying ourselves with the Body of Christ. We had some sermons by the chaplain of the boat and some by our Reverend Fathers. We prayed four times a day: at four o'clock and again at eight o'clock in the morning, at five o'clock and eight o'clock in the evening. We sang the solemn Mass and Vespers every Sunday and on the feast days. As I told you, we arrived on the Tropic on Good Friday, and now I will tell you of our observance of that day. After the reading of the Passion, we had the adoration of the Cross in a very solemn and devout way. We were the first ones adoring the Cross, barefooted, followed by the Reverend Fathers, the officers, the passengers, and the ship's crew, all in a very respectful way. During the season of the celebration of the Blessed Sacrament we had a procession around the capstan. On a vessel, if the officers are devout, all the crew will follow their example. We never miss ringing the bell and saying the Angelus four times a day. Now, let me return to our voyage.

The day after we had lost sight of the enemy vessel, the sea was so agitated that it continued to make us fearful. It was sometimes so rough that it was impossible for us to remain in bed. We needed ropes to keep us from falling. We held on without stopping, sometimes on one side, sometimes on the other, and always holding firm somewhere. But we suffered still more from the length of the voyage, ardently longing more and more for the promised land of Louisiana. Every day we redoubled our petitions to obtain more favorable weather. The Lord granted us, by intervals, some hours of good weather. With His help we arrived at Caille St. Louis, a port on the Island of Saint

Domingue, where we anchored.[26] (See fig. 2.) It was there that
we became acquainted with the Monsieurs Mosquitoes, little
animals that I can compare to the ones called bibets or gnats
in France, except that their bite is more poisonous and more
painful. They cause blisters and violent itching. They take away
the skin, and then ulcers come when one scratches. The animals
sting with such force that we had our faces and hands covered
with their marks, but, happily, these insects appear only in the
evening after the sun goes down. They reappear the next day
at sunset.

Since there was not a religious house or anybody that
we knew, we disembarked to take care of our laundry, which
needed to be washed and bleached. On the evening that the
boat anchored, the gentleman of the Company came to visit
us and put the ship store at our disposal. We could not refuse
this gracious offer since it was necessary for us to leave the ship.
Our Reverend Mother promised them that on the next day
she would have the honor with all the Community of paying
respects to the two gentlemen on land. The two gentlemen are
of true merit and known for exemplary conduct and politeness.
The first one was called Cirou. He is still unmarried, a man
full of spirit, who is reputed to be very good. He conducts an
agreeable conversation, in spite of his continual preoccupation
with business. The second one, who is of equal merit, was called
Girard. We ate at their home with a young Creole lady of the
country, whose manners could be likened to any Parisian lady

26. The port that Hachard calls *Caille St. Louis* was more commonly known as
Les Cayes. Located on the south coast of the island, it was a frequent port of call for
French ships bound for Louisiana in the eighteenth century.

of the highest caliber.[27] We cannot add anything in praise of the graciousness that these gentlemen extended to us. From the first day on and the rest of the time, that we remained at their home, which was about fifteen days, they treated us magnificently and with utmost propriety and abundance.

Two days after our arrival, the governor inquired about the state of our health and came after dinner to pay us a visit. His name is Monsieur de Brache, a man of quality and great wealth. He spoke to us of an earth tremor that had struck the place that morning. It was only I, of all the Community, who had noticed it, without knowing what it was. I regarded the shaking as if I imagined that I was still on the *Gironde*. This Governor invited us to dinner at his home twice, and we dined in an exquisite French manner. We were very happy at this home, and we had complete liberty there. We performed our spiritual exercises with more ease than we did on the boat.

The Governor told us that he wanted to have a house of Ursulines in this country. (Nobody could finance one better than he. He does not have children and has 50,000 livres income.) Messieurs Cirou and Girard had the same desire for the education of young Creoles, who are naturally of a happy disposition. It is necessary to send them to France to the Communities for instruction. There is hope that we will someday have a house of our order in this country. They wanted information as to how to proceed at the Court of France to obtain such permission. We gave them a brief instruction in writing. If they obtain this

---

27. In the eighteenth century, a Creole was a person born in the New World of Old World ancestry, either European, African, or a mixture of the two.

permission from the King, I have no doubt that they will have an infinite number of holy Religious who, full of zeal for the salvation of souls, will come willingly to spread the sacred fire of the love of God. If people only knew what it was to have the burning zeal of the love of God, they would wish ardently to be consumed by this fire. The one thing that will really excite the zeal to serve in this country is the lack of religion in this place. The more devout are the ones who do not lead scandalous lives publicly. In all the country, there is only one priest, who has to say Mass twice on all Sundays and feast days, the High Mass in the parish of which he is the pastor, and a second Mass at Fort St. Louis, where a great number of officers and soldiers are stationed to keep guard, and which is situated in the middle of the sea. Monsieur de Brache is the commander there, but since he does not go there often, it is the commanding officer who presides in his stead. The pastor resides in this place. The governor wished and asked us to go to see this fort, which, according to those in the know, is a very rare occurrence. We found there three companies of handsome troops, under arms, who were lined up to honor us with the sound of drums. Before we departed, they presented us with some refreshments.

Finally, we set sail on the nineteenth of May, overwhelmed with kindness and presents from Monsieur Cirou and Monsieur Girard, who gave us, among other things, a barrel of sugar weighing 300 pounds. They gave as much to our Reverend Fathers, no doubt to sweeten the remainder of the journey for us, which still had some five hundred leagues remaining. The wind was at first very favorable, but it was so for only a short time. We encountered calm waters alternating with high winds. Then we met three pirate ships, two of which caused us alarm.[28] They circled our vessel for two days, not daring to attack us. We had to be always ready to defend ourselves. They lowered a number of people of questionable appearance who said they were of English nationality into small boats, and they came to us pretending to want to buy some wine. Our commanders knew that they came only to reconnoiter the state of our vessel and the crew. We thought to imprison them or shoot at their boat to send them to the bottom of the sea, but we gave them grace. We were content to tell them to return to their ship immediately. They obeyed and left without asking anything else.

We hoped that, in spite of all the difficulties, we would arrive around the Feast of Corpus Christi, but Our Lord, Who had reserved the greatest trial for the end, sent us violent contrary winds that, together with the currents of the Gulf of Mexico, drove us instead to the island called "White." Since we were impatient to have the first sighting of the Mississippi, we felt great joy when we were near this island, but, dear God, it was a short-lived joy at a high price. After dinner, we went to pass time on the deck, and when we least expected it, our boat all of a sudden went aground with a sudden jolt. We felt that we were lost, without recourse. We took out our rosary and said our *In manus,* thinking that all was done and that we would make our religious establishment right there.[29] (See fig. 3)

28. At this point in the French original, Hachard switches to the term *Forban* to describe pirate vessels. The term is derived from the French word for *banned* and refers to persons banned from their countries of birth, that is, outlaws.

29. The *In manus* is the prayer recited at the point of death, beginning, "Into your hands I commend my spirit, O Lord."

The commanders stopped eating their dinner. Whereas the Reverend Fathers and we ate at eleven o'clock, they dined after us, at noon. We had supper at five o'clock and our officers at six o'clock. All the crew was immediately in motion. They raised the sail and did everything possible to pull us out of the bad situation. Everything was useless. Someone ascertained that the boat was mired in more than five feet of sand. In fact, the boat had already made its bed, and the only movement was by the rudder, which from time to time jerked, making us tremble. Finally our captain decided to unload the boat. They began with the cannons, which were put on two pieces of wood to keep them from sinking. They took them far, and they abandoned them to the sea. Then, they emptied out the ballast, which was composed of gravel and lead and iron; all was thrown into the sea. Since that was not enough to raise the boat, they considered also jettisoning the passenger baggage that was stowed between decks. Ours was the first in line, so it was up to us to make the first sacrifice. We did not take long to be resolved to this and we consented, with all our hearts, to be deprived of everything and feel the greatest poverty. The officers assured us that there was no need to fear for our lives, because we were very close to land. But we should disembark only under extreme necessity because this island was inhabited by savages who, they said, were very cruel.[30] Not only did they eat white people, but they made them suffer with torments a thousand times worse than death. Sometimes, they made them drink their own blood and

30. The eighteenth-century French called the natives of the Americas *sauvages,* and this has been translated as *savages* rather than the anachronistic terms *Indians* or *Native Americans.*

made them suffer the most cruel martyrdoms. It is true that if we had been in great need of leaving the boat, we would have numbered, crew and passengers, a true little army that, with the firearms that the savages feared greatly, we would have been safe from all abuse, but we would still have been at risk of dying from hunger.

Finally, when we believed that our baggage would be thrown into the sea, the commander changed his mind and had all the sugar thrown overboard instead. There was a great quantity of sugar sacks in the ship. This was done. Our Reverend Fathers and we lost the two barrels, each one weighing 300 pounds, which Monsieur Cirou and Monsieur Girard had given to us when we left Caille. This did not do any good, so they wanted again to throw over the baggage chests, but by God's permission and the protection of the Blessed Mother, whom we were petitioning each time they were preparing to jettison our luggage, the captain would change his mind and throw over something else. They threw over sixty-one barrels of wine and a quantity of ballast and iron pieces that they found. This sad work was executed during the night. We were on the deck to watch with pity this poor house cleaning. It was the desolation of desolations to see the poor passengers who trembled for their belongings and grieved over the sugar. No one was exempt, not even the officers, who had some as well. All the sugar was thrown into the sea without distinguishing to whom it belonged. The wine belonging to the Company along with a great number of packages was also thrown into the sea. After that, new efforts were made to dislodge the vessel, and they were successful, which filled us with joy. This first danger lasted from noon to about ten to eleven o'clock the next morning. Nobody went to bed that night; however, they anchored the boat and decided not to leave until the tide would return a few hours later. Then we began sailing.

We had traveled only a quarter of a league, and we had not recovered from our fear when the ship touched ground for the second time. But it was with such a series of jolts that our only hope was in the power of God. Even our commanders were surprised that the ship had withstood the jolt. They said that of ten ships, nine would have been destroyed at the first jolt. The ship must have been constructed of iron. They did not speak anymore of going down to land. Besides, one could not see land except at a far distance. All the sailors were dismayed and were in the launch and the dinghy with some anchors to pull the ship from the back. They hardly had time to think of the danger that they were in, because they had to work without stopping.

I confess to you, my dear Father, that I neither thought of nor have seen death so close; although I always trusted in the help of the Blessed Mother. Fear was painted on all the faces and in the hearts of even the most confident. All in agreement made a vow, each a different one because we were in such a state of trouble and alarm, that we could not agree on which saint to petition. However, each one hid the fear and only thought of their own final end. The first place one came to, one knelt down to pray, most often at the feet of our kind superior, who made clear to us that we would suffer less pain than the others if we died because we had made, before sailing, a perfect sacrifice of our lives to the Lord. I shall not recount all that she said to us to give us strength, I can only add that her words encouraged us infinitely. Her example alone gave us a peaceful courage to face death. She held onto her spirit of sacrifice with an amazing liberty, but the Lord was content this time with our good will. He gave his blessing to the care of our commanders and to the work of our sailors and passengers, who did not spare themselves. Among them were our Reverend Fathers, as well as Brother Crucy, who distinguished themselves. Our vessel was once more pulled free, and what was more astonishing was that it was not damaged, at least not visibly. Before God, we have to thank Monsieur Dusaillet, General Director of the Company and Commandant of Lorient, who had given all his attention to putting our vessel in good condition before we undertook our voyage.

After this accident, the rowboat always went before us with a depth probe in the hand of an officer until we were well out. That put us fifteen leagues away from our destination. This delay was troublesome because we had little water. There were already days in which we were reduced to a pint of water per day. It was the same with wine. The heat was so stifling, and the measure of drink was less than in Rouen. We suffered much from thirst, and that made us exchange our wine for water; however they only gave us a bottle of water for a bottle of wine. Even then, we were happy to have water at that price. This situation lasted more than fifteen days, because the wind continued to be contrary, and the waves took us off course. We were obliged to use the anchor several times a day.

We finally spotted land, but since it was unknown to us, it was only our need for water that made us go closer. The rowboat, steered by our Second Captain, was sent ahead of us to try to ascertain where we were. The closer we approached, the more we were persuaded that this island was inhabited only by savages. We came to this conclusion because we saw great fires during the night. However, less than two hours after the rowboat departed, the winds became favorable. Our First Captain did not want to waste this opportunity to proceed on our way. He had the cannon fired to inform the rowboat crew to rejoin us. At the same time, he raised the anchor to continue on our way, hoping that the rowboat, having heard the signal, would return immediately. But he was mistaken, for the Second Captain mistook this cannon shot for thunder and continued on his way toward land, getting further from us than three leagues. After the wind let off, we lowered the anchor to wait for the rowboat, which we were anxious to see. We waited impatiently. The wind was entirely against the rowboat, and the sea in extraordinary agitation. Everything made us fear for him. We did not have the joy of seeing him again until the next morning, and at that time they put the sloop into the ocean to get some fresh water from the island, which we believed was the Island of St. Rose.

We remained anchored there for three or four days waiting for favorable winds. During this time our Second Captain, who had departed in the sloop and who was unsuccessful in finding fresh water on this island, had a hole dug on the shore. There he found drinking water and filled several barrels that were brought to our ship. We were very happy because we were beginning to run out. The wind changed and became favorable. We raised anchor and continued on our way. After a few days, we came to Dauphine Island and the same time, a brigantine approached us. Since we only expected friends, the sight of it brought us great joy, hoping to get news from New Orleans in this way. Our hope was not in vain. We had the pleasure to see a brigantine whose captain was a friend of ours. He asked to greet us, and it was from him that we had news of Reverend Father de Beaubois, who was anxiously awaiting us. Everything was ready to receive us. Our lodging was ready, and they were waiting for our monastery to be completed. I assure you, my dear Father, that it was the first real joy that we felt since our departure. It was so great, that it made us forget all the hardships we had encountered.

Accompanied by the brigantine, we continued on our way toward Dauphine Island intending to get some water. But, since the wind was favorable, we kept on our way and headed to Belize, where we arrived July 23, five months to the day since our departure. Far from Rouen, about 2,400 leagues, it is a port located at the entrance of the Mississippi River on the western shore. Monsieur Duvergé is in charge there for the Company. Right away he came on board to see us and to offer his house, while we waited for some conveyance to take us up river to New Orleans. We accepted his offer, and on the twenty-sixth, the Feast of St. Ann, we boarded a boat with some of our necessary baggage. Monsieur Duvergé came to take us there, and it was good, because the weather was very inclement. The wind was contrary, and our boat was loaded very heavily, and worst of all our sailors were cursing and for no reason. We found ourselves in great danger from which we would not have escaped had Monsieur Duvergé not obliged them to stop on a little island called the Island of the Canons, situated at the mouth of the Mississippi River, a little way up the river. This island is no bigger than half an acre, but it commands the whole mouth of the river. We had trouble getting ashore because we kept getting stuck. We had never in our lives heard anybody swearing as much as our crew. We were in danger of spending the night on this island, where there were a dozen workers of the Company, who were working on the construction of a kind of fort under the command of Monsieur Duvergé. He sent his workers to find some pirogues for us and raised a banner to inform Belize that he was there and that he wanted some conveyances. These pirogues are hollowed out of trees, which are sometimes big enough to hold sixteen persons. The three pirogues that took us were smaller. We had to separate ourselves into two groups. The third pirogue held Monsieur Duvergé and Father Doutreleau.

It was in this way that we arrived in Belize at the house of Monsieur Duvergé. He treated us as well as he possibly could. This gentleman is very gracious, and although young and without a wife, he leads a good life and quite alone. Since he is dedicated without pause to the business confided in him, we are convinced that the Company has few employees as dedicated as this gentleman. We have reason to believe that he either has enemies, (true virtue is always persecuted) or that he is not very well known by the directors of the Company, for if they knew him better, without doubt, they would have promoted him. It would be a pleasure and a duty for these gentlemen to recognize true merit. The merit of Monsieur Duvergé seems to us worthy of the most important position.

We remained at his home until the twenty-ninth of the same month, waiting for news from New Orleans. Father Tartarin had gone ahead of us. He departed from the *Gironde* some days before us to announce our coming to Father de Beaubois, whom he pleasantly surprised with his arrival. Our long voyage had alarmed the whole country, and many people believed us to be lost. Father de Beaubois immediately sent a sloop and some pirogues for us. Since he was convalescing from illness and not in a condition to meet us himself, he sent Monsieur Massy, brother of our postulant. This gentleman brought Reverend Mother Superior a letter from Monsieur Perier, governor and Knight of St. Louis, and another letter from Monsieur Delachaise, general director of the Company. These two gentlemen waited anxiously to see us.

The sloop was too small to hold the number of our company. We had to separate. Our Reverend Mother Superior chose to be in the pirogue with the youngest of her daughters. I was in this number, accompanied by Reverend Father Doutreleau and Brother Crucy. The rest of the Mothers were in the sloop with Monsieur Massy and our two servants. There was still a little pirogue for the domestics and workers of the Reverend Fathers. We must acknowledge that all the hardships of the *Gironde* were nothing compared to what we had in this little crossing, which is only thirty leagues upriver, from Belize to New Orleans. This journey, which ordinarily takes six days, took us seven days, because we wanted to keep pace with the sloop, but since the sloop was very slow, we went ahead, and we arrived a day sooner than the others. We departed Belize on St. Ignatius' Day, and the sloop arrived on the day of the Octave. What made this crossing so tiring was that every evening we had to prepare a sleeping tent. We had to do it an hour before the sun sets, in order to have time to prepare the place and to have supper, because as soon as the sun set, the mosquitoes swarmed on us, similar to those that we began to see at the Caille St. Louis. Their comrades, called "Frappes d'abord," which one sees better because they are big, are equally bad. Sometimes they come in such great numbers that one could cut them with a knife, but they are as unmerciful as the mosquitoes. They both sting without mercy and their stings are very bad. All along the river there is no cultivated land. There are only big savage wild woods, inhabited only by wildlife of all colors—serpents, snakes, scorpions, crocodiles, vipers, ticks, and frogs and others that did us no harm, though they got very close to us. We saw all sorts and in great numbers. The weeds are so high in this place that we could only set our tents on the shore of the river. To make the sleeping place, our sailors put cane in the form of a cradle around a mattress and enclosed us two by two in our tents where we lay down all fully dressed. Then they covered the cradle with a big cloth, so that the mosquitoes and the Frappes d'abord would not be able to find even a little passage to come to visit us.

Twice we lay down in the middle of the mud, and the rain that fell from the sky in abundance soaked us as well as our mattresses, which were nearly swimming in water. Thunder and lightening had come in the middle of the night. The next day the pirogue could not advance, because it, as well as our habits and our mattresses, was soaked. On this occasion, several of our Mothers were very uncomfortable. Some had colds, and others had respiratory problems. Others had swollen faces and legs. One of them had a more serious illness. As for me, although I had been equally bathed, I was not indisposed.

Besides this, we also had trouble with the pirogues. We could not sit, stand, or kneel. And still, we were not allowed to move about because the pirogues would have capsized, and we would have become food for the fish. All our baggage of mattresses and chests filled it up and we had to be on top on a little board, and when the pirogue stopped, we changed position. We ate hardtack and cured meat that came from the *Gironde* that our pirogue master cooked for us in a pot. All these little troubles bothered us at the time, but one is well recompensed later by the pleasure one has in recounting each of these little adventures. One is surprised when one considers the strength and the courage God provides on these occasions. That proves that He never abandons anyone, and that He does not permit us to be tempted above our strength, giving us grace in proportion to the trials put before us. It is true that the ardent desire that we had to arrive at this Promised Land made us endure our trials with joy.

When we were eight to ten leagues from New Orleans, we began to encounter the inhabitants. Each of them wanted us to stop and to come into their homes. We were received everywhere with expressions of joy, and we found a great number of honest people, who had come from France and from Canada to establish themselves in this country. Everywhere they promised us boarders, and several people wanted to give them to us right then and there.[31] Our last night was spent in the house of Mon-

---

31. Boarding students, called *pensionnaires,* were an important source of income for the Ursulines in France and would become their principal source of revenue in colonial Louisiana.

sieur Massy, brother of our postulant, where we were as comfortable as at home. We had hoped to relax there a few days, but Reverend Father Tartarin came with Monsieur Delachaise's son and told us that the Reverend Father de Beaubois was awaiting us the next morning very early. So, we re-embarked at three o'clock in the morning and we arrived at five o'clock in New Orleans. (See fig. 4.)

It would be too long and even useless to express to you, my dear Father, our joy at the sight of the land, for which we had longed for such a long time and how great our consolation when we set foot on land. We found very few people in the port because of the early hour. Therefore, we walked without embarrassment to the house of Reverend Father de Beaubois. We soon encountered him, coming to meet us with great joy because the delay of our arrival had caused him much concern. He imagined that we had perished on the way, all the more because the trip ordinarily takes three months when the wind is a little favorable, and we had taken five because of contrary winds. He took us to his home, and, after some relaxation, he presented us with a very good breakfast, which was interrupted by a great number of his friends, who came to greet us and in whose company we were led to our home at about ten or eleven o'clock in the morning.

This is a house that the Company rents for fifteen hundred pounds a year, to lodge us while awaiting the completion of our monastery. It is located directly at the end of the city, and the house that they are building for us is at the other end. We do not expect to take possession of our monastery and the hospital for a year, or perhaps longer, for the workers are not as numerous here as in France, especially since they want to construct it to last; all will be in brick. While waiting, they built us a small lodging area in our residence for extern students and for lodging the boarders. The owner of the house furnished the wood, we the workers. There are already more than thirty boarders from here and Belize and the surrounding area who insisted on being received. The parents are carried away with joy to see us, saying that they no longer worry that they will return to France since they have here what they need to educate their daughters. This good disposition of the inhabitants makes them attentive to our needs. They compete with each other as to who can provide the most. This puts us under obligation to almost everybody here.

Monsieur Perier, commander, and Madame, his wife, came specifically to see us.[32] They are very sociable persons of great merit. In three months, this gentleman earned the esteem of all the country. There is nothing objectionable in his conduct. He concerns himself with matters of justice for the interest of the Company in a quiet manner. He has brought peace to the troubles of disunion that existed in this city. He has established a very well organized police force. He declares war on vice and drives off those who live a scandalous life. There is corporal punishment for girls who lead immoral lives. The trial process ends in three or four days. They hang or break on the wheel for the least theft. The Council is sovereign; there is no appeal here. They bring prisoners here from the Illinois country, 400

---

32. In the earliest published version of the letters, the name is given as *Monsieur Paris*. This is an error, made either by Hachard or by the printer.

leagues away. That is not to say that there are no judges there, but appeals are made here.[33]

We also received many kindnesses from Monsieur Delachaise, general director of the Company. He has refused us nothing of what we have asked of him.

We hope that our establishment will be for the glory of God and that, in time, it will produce great good for the salvation of souls. This has been our principal aim. If one knew how sweet it is to suffer for Jesus Christ, with the hope of gaining for Him the souls that He redeemed at the price of His blood, I do not doubt that a great number of holy religious sisters would follow our example and offer themselves for the establishment of the convent of our order which could be done, as I remarked, at Caille St. Louis. Or at least, volunteers could come to join us if later we still need some religious to help us teach and convert these poor savages. The length and trials of the voyage deter no one. If one knows how much the Lord magnificently compensates those who do this for him, one would count all this as nothing or as an insignificant thing. I will say from my own experience that the Lord is pleased to let the strength of his arm strike through His weakest subjects.

Since the day after our arrival, we have the Mass said here every day by Reverend Father de Beaubois, and for three weeks

33. Hachard is referring to the Louisiana Superior Council, a governing body for the colony that exercised both legislative and judicial authority over the Lower Mississippi Valley. People could be tried by lesser authorities in the Illinois Country, but if a person appealed that decision, he or she did so before the Superior Council in New Orleans, whose decision was final. There could be no direct appeal, for example, to the French crown.

prior to yesterday, the 26th of October, we have had the Blessed Sacrament in the tabernacle, which we had made here. May He be adored, loved, glorified and respected all over the earth, and may He give all of us His holy blessing.

I have the honor to be with all possible respect,

My dear father,

Your most humble and very obedient daughter and servant, Marie Madeleine Hachard of St. Stanislaus.

New Orleans

January 1, 1728

My Dear Father,

I have just learned that the vessel called *Deux Frères* is going to depart for France. I take advantage of this occasion to wish you, as well as my dear mother, brothers and sisters, a good and happy new year. I pray each day to the Lord to keep you in perfect health.

You must have received a package of my letters with an account of all our voyage, which I sent you this past twenty-seventh of October, by the ship named *Prince de Conty*. You asked me in all your letters not to let any occasion go by without writing you. It is my duty. I obey you, and I will take care to satisfy your request exactly.

All our community is in perfect health. At present we have nine boarders. We will receive as many more after Epiphany, and we will also instruct a number of day students.

They are working very hard on our house. Monsieur Perier, our Commandant, always willing to do what he can to please us, promised us that we would be able to move in before a year's lapse. The engineer came yesterday to show us the plans. We desire nothing as much as to see ourselves in this house, finally to be occupied also at the hospital to serve the sick. We learn every day that it is the greatest pity in the world to see the bad situation there and that the greatest number of sick die without care.

The intention of the Commandant and of the principal inhabitants of this city is that we would also take the girls and the women of bad conduct. That is not yet determined on our side, but they let us hear that it would be a great good for the colony. And for that, they propose to build for us a special apartment at the end of our enclosure to incarcerate those people.

We also have a class to instruct the women and girls among the blacks and savages. They come every day from one o'clock in the afternoon until two-thirty. You see, my dear Father, that we are not useless in this country. I assure you that all our moments are counted and that we do not have one for ourselves. We are taking care of a little orphan girl, who was a servant in a house where she was not given a very good example. It is still the intention of Reverend Father de Beaubois that we take care of little orphan girls through charity, and to encourage us, he tells us that he and Monsieur Perier will take charge of all the orphan boys.

Finally, we are determined to spare ourselves nothing in all that could be for the greater glory of God. I am sometimes employed with the day students. I cannot express to you the pleasure that I find in instructing their little souls and teaching them to know and to love God. I pray the Lord will give me His grace to succeed in this.

In a few years we may need some sisters to come from France, since we may not be able to do everything. When we have absolute necessity, we will ask for them.

Our Reverend Mother Superior has a thousand kindnesses for me. She, as well as Mother St. Francis Xavier, whom you saw in Rouen, send you greetings.

All our community is so happy that it cannot be expressed. We are going to follow, all at the same time, the functions of four different communities, that of the Ursulines, our first and principal order, that of the hospitalieres, that of the St. Josephs and that of the Refuge.[34] We shall try to fulfill each as faithfully as will be possible.

I beg you to believe in my sincere and respectful attachment.

My dear Father,

Your very humble and very obedient daughter and servant,

Hachard of St. Stanislaus

New Orleans

April 24, 1728

My very dear Father,

I received with much pleasure the letter that you had the goodness to write to me, dated the twelfth and twentieth of August 1727. You asked for an explanation of the state of the

---

34. Each religious order or type of religious institution in this period provided a single type of social service. The Ursulines were educators; the hospitaliers were nurses; the Sisters of St. Joseph sheltered orphans; and "the Refuge" was the name given to institutions that housed delinquent and/or abandoned women and girls. Hachard may be referring here to the Order of Our Lady of Charity of the Refuge, which was founded in France in 1641.

country, the situation of our city, and finally everything that one can learn of these places. I hope to have sufficiently foreseen your intention by the detailed account of our little adventures during all of our voyage and our arrival here, which I sent you in the month of October 1727, and by several letters that I had the honor of writing to you.

I believe that I told you that our city, named New Orleans, capital of all Louisiana, is situated on the shore of the Mississippi River, on the east side. It is, in this place, larger than the River Seine in Rouen. On our side of this river is a well-constructed levee to prevent the overflowing of the river into the city. And along this embankment, at the side of the city, is a big ditch to collect the water that might overflow it, with palisades of wood to close it.

On the other side of this river are wild woods in which there are some little cabins where the slaves of the Company of the Indies live. You see by this that the map of the state of Louisiana, which you told me you had bought, in which the city of New Orleans is represented as being situated on the shore of a lake named Pontchartrain, a distance of six leagues from the Mississippi River, is not correct. Our city is not situated on the shore of a lake, but rather on the shore of the Mississippi River. It is true that all the force of the river does not flow by here, for above our city the river separates to form three branches of the river that join below and empty themselves rapidly into the Gulf of Mexico.

Our city is very beautiful, well constructed and regularly built, as much as I am able to know of it from what I saw the day of our arrival in this land. Since that day, we have always remained in our cloister. Before our arrival we were given a very bad idea of the city. It is true that those who spoke to us of this had not been here for several years. They have worked, and they continue to work, to improve the city.

The streets are very wide and laid out in lines. The main street measures a league in length. The houses are very well constructed in collombage and mortar, whitewashed, paneled, and sunlit. The roofs of the houses are covered with little flat plates made of wood cut in the form of slate. One must know this, in order to believe it, for this covering has all the appearance and beauty of slate. It is enough to tell you that here one publicly sings a song in which there is only this city which resembles the city of Paris. This tells you everything.

In effect, it is a very beautiful city. If I do not have enough eloquence to describe to you the beauty expressed in the song, it is because I find a difference between this city and the city of Paris. One could persuade people who have never seen the capitol of France, but I saw it, and the song will not persuade me to the contrary of what I think. It is true that the city grows every day and could become as beautiful and large as the principal cities of France, if workers come again and the population grows in proportion to its size.

The women are ignorant of their welfare, but not of their vanity. The luxury in this city makes no distinctions of persons; all are of equal magnificence. Most of them, along with their family, are reduced to living on nothing but sagamité, which is a kind of gruel. They are dressed in velvet and satin cloth or damasks full of ribbons, in spite of the cost, for these fabrics sell regularly in this country for three times more than in France. The women here, as women everywhere, wear white powder and rouge to hide the wrinkles on their faces, and beauty spots. In the end, the devil has a great empire here, but this does not take away from us the hope of destroying him, with God's love. There is an infinity of examples to make his strength show through our weakness. The more powerful the enemy is, the more we are encouraged to fight him. What pleases us is the docility of the children, whom one forms as one wants. The blacks are also easy to instruct once they learn to speak French. It is not the same for the savages, whom one does not baptize without trembling because of the tendency they have to sin, especially the women, who, under a modest air, hide the passions of beasts.

Since our arrival, our residence has been the most beautiful house in the city. It has two floors, and over it is a Mansard roof. We have there all the necessary apartments. Six doors enter the lower apartments. Everywhere are large openings, but no glass. The openings are all covered with fine and light cloth, which admits as much daylight as glass.

It is situated at the end of the city. We have a courtyard and a garden, which adjoin each other on one side, and at the end are wild trees of prodigious height and girth. This makes us among the first for an infinite number of visits from mosquitoes and the Frappes d'abord, and a type of flies or gnats whose species I still do not know. I know them neither by their first nor last names. I only see them, for at this moment, there are several flying around me that would like to attack me. These bad insects sting without mercy. We are assaulted by them at night. Happily, they appear only in the evening after sunset until the next morning, when they return to the woods. This obliges us to close our doors and windows securely at night, otherwise, they will not fail to come to see us in our beds. Whatever precautions we take, we are unable to escape carrying their marks.

The house that is being constructed for us is situated at the other end of the city. Reverend Father de Beaubois and the engineer of the Company who designed it, follow the instructions that we gave them, and they often show us the plans. It will be entirely of brick and large enough to lodge a great community. It will have all the rooms that we could wish, very regularly built, well paneled, with large openings and glass in the frames. But it scarcely advances. Monsieur Perier, our Governor and Commandant, gave us the hope that it would be ready by year's end, but workers being so rare, we would be happy to be able to lodge there and to take possession of our hospital by Easter of 1729. Then we will need more help. I pray to the Lord to send us good people.

Monsieur Perier and Madame, his wife, who is very amiable and very pious, do us the honor of coming to see us often. The Lieutenant of the King is also a perfect gentleman and a former officer. All overwhelm us with all kinds of presents. They gave us two cows with their calves, a sow and its little ones, chickens, and Muscovy ducks. All of these are beginning to fill our animal enclosure. We also have there some turkeys and some geese. The inhabitants, seeing that we do not want to take any money for instructing the day students, are filled with gratitude and help us in every way they can. The marks of protection that we receive from the leading inhabitants of the country make us respected by everyone. All that will not continue if our actions do not confirm their high regard for us.

During Lent, we eat meat four days a week, as permitted by the Church. Other than during Lent, we fast only on Fridays. We drink beer. Our most common food is rice with milk, little wild beans, meat, and fish. But in the summer we eat little meat. They slaughter only twice a week. It is not easy to preserve. Hunting lasts all winter, which begins in the month of October. It is done ten miles from our city. They hunt wild cattle in great number, which they bring here and to the surrounding area. We buy the meat, such as venison, for three sols per pound. This meat is better than beef or mutton that you eat in Rouen.

The wild ducks are very cheap here. Teals, waterfowl, geese, and other fowl and game are very common. We hardly buy any, for we do not want to indulge ourselves. Finally, it is a charming country all during winter, and in the summer, fish is very abundant and very good. There are oysters and carp of prodigious size which are delicious. In regard to other fish, there are none of this kind in France. There are large monstrous fish that are good enough. We also eat watermelons and French melons, and potatoes, which are large roots that one cooks in the ashes like chestnuts. These taste good, but sweeter, softer, and very good. All of this, my dear Father, is just as I report it to you, I do not tell you anything of which I have not had experience. Here they eat many other kinds of meat, fish, and vegetables that I have not yet tasted, and I cannot tell you of their goodness.

As for the fruits of the country, there are many that we do not find very excellent, except the peaches and the figs, which are here in abundance. They send us such great quantities of these from the habitations that we have made preserves, and the jelly of the blackberries is very good. Reverend Father de Beaubois has the most beautiful garden in the city. It is full of orange trees, which bear oranges as beautiful and sweet as the ones in Cap Français. He gave us three hundred sour ones that we preserved. Thank God, we are not in need of anything. Our Reverend Father takes care to furnish us with our food. We fare much better than we believed we would, but that is neither our wish nor the intention of our enterprise. Our principal aim is to gain souls for the Lord, and He gives us the grace to succeed. Our Reverend Father aids us well in this. He says Holy Mass for us every day and gives us public talks. If we had the misfortune to lose him, through sickness or otherwise, we would be very saddened and most pitiable.

This Reverend Father gave us a retreat during Holy Week and our boarders and several ladies of the city attended assiduously. Nearly 200 in number were to be found sometimes at the exhortations and talks. We had the lessons of *Tenebre* in music, and a *Miserere,* accompanied by instruments, every day.[35] Our Mother assistant, who is Madame Le Boulenger, distinguished herself on this occasion. On Easter Sunday, during Mass and the benediction of the Blessed Sacrament, we sang motets in four voices, and on the last of the Easter feast days we sang the

35. *Tenebre* is the name that has been given to the service of Matins and Lauds on the three days before Easter. These services take place during the night, and the candles are extinguished at the conclusion of services on these three days, leaving the worshippers in darkness to commemorate the death of Jesus. The *Miserere* is a prayer that takes as its text Psalm 51. The first line, in Latin Vulgate, is "Miserere mei, Domine"; in English, "Have mercy on me, O God."

entire mass with music. The convents in France, with all their fame, do not do as much.

All this makes a good impression and helps very much in attracting the public, some out of the beginnings of devotion, others out of curiosity. It is always followed by a sermon at the end, for the Reverend Father has an admirable zeal. It seems that he has undertaken to, and it is certain that he will, convert everyone. But I assure you, my dear Father, that there is much work to succeed in that, for not only do debauchery, bad faith and all the other vices reign here more than in any other place, but they do so in abundance. As for the girls of bad conduct, they are closely observed here and severely punished by putting them on a wooden horse and whipped by all the soldiers of the regiment that guards our city. This does not prevent there from being more than would fill a reformatory. The trial of a thief is completed in two days. He is hung or broken on the wheel, be he white, savage, or black there is no distinction or mercy.

Our little community grows from day to day. We have twenty boarders, of whom eight today made their first communion, three ladies also board, and three orphans that we took through charity. We also have seven slave boarders to instruct for baptism and first communion, besides a great number of day students, female blacks and female savages who come for two hours a day for instruction.[36] The custom here is to

36. Here Hachard uses the words for *slave* and *black* in the French original: "esclaves pensionnaires" (slave boarders) and "nègresses & sauvagesses" (blacks and savages). There is no surviving evidence from the 1720s to suggest who the slave boarders that Hachard mentions were and by whom their boarding fees were paid. There is a case from the 1730s that suggests that at least some of the slave boarders may have been the progeny of white men and enslaved women. In 1737 the Ursulines

marry the girls from age twelve to fourteen. Before our arrival, many married before they even knew how many Gods there are. Judge the rest. But since we have been here, none of them have been married without having come to receive our instructions.

We are accustomed to seeing people who are completely black. A few days ago, they gave us two black boarders aged six and seventeen to instruct in our religion, and they will remain here to serve us. If it were the fashion here, black women would wear beauty marks on their faces. They would have to be given white ones, which would create quite a funny effect.

You see, my dear Father, the sorts of things upon which we can exercise our zeal. I cannot tell you the pleasure that we get from instructing all these young people. It is enough for us to consider the needs that they have. The boarders, ranging from twelve to fifteen years of age, have never been to Confession or even to Mass. They were raised on their habitations, five to six leagues from this city, and in consequence without any spiritual succor. They had never heard anyone speak of God. When we tell them the most common things, for them they are oracles that come out of our mouths. We have the consolation to find in them great docility and a strong desire to be instructed. All would like to be nuns, which is not to the liking of Reverend

------

petitioned the Superior Council for the boarding fees owed by a "mulatress" who was placed with them in 1735. The petition suggested that the debt be paid out of the estate of a man named St. Julien because the mixed-race girl was property belonging to the estate of the debtor. Petition to Sr. de Salmon by Sister St. André, July 29, 1737, Records of the Louisiana Superior Council, Louisiana State Historical Center, New Orleans.

de Beaubois, our very worthy superior. He finds it more proper for them to become Christian mothers who, by their good example, will finally establish religion in the country.

I am always very happy to be in this country and in my vocation. And what doubles my joy is to see the time of my profession draw near.[37] I cannot tell you the joy I will have to pronounce my vows in a foreign land where Christianity is almost unknown. It is true that there are many good people by worldly terms, but here there is not the least appearance of devotion, nor of Christianity. How happy we would be if we could establish it here, with the help of our Reverend Father Superior and some Capuchin friars, who are similarly employed and do all that is possible. I assure you that we will spare nothing.

I must tell you of the sad adventure that befell our two Reverend Fathers Tartarin and Doutreleau, worthy leaders of our voyage. We have just learned from their letters that twenty leagues from Illinois, the canoe that carried Reverend Father Doutreleau was destroyed during the river crossing. He saved himself by swimming, wearing nothing but his shirt. He lost everything for his chapel, his clothes, and all of his baggage. He had traveled 500 leagues happily just to be shipwrecked thus at the end. Nothing happened to Reverend Father Tartarin, who was in another canoe and who, having two cassocks, gave him one in charity.

37. Hachard is speaking of the ceremony at which she would take her final vows. On this occasion, the novice professed her commitment to the religious life and pronounced her solemn vows before the convent community and a priest, hence the ceremony's name.

Almost without thinking, here I am led up to Illinois. I will tell you, my dear Father, that Reverend Boulenger, who is there, asked for nuns to form an establishment there. He wrote for that reason to Mother Boulenger, his sister, who answered him that she had not yet enough vocations to spread beyond New Orleans, and that it may be possible for some to come in a few years. However, she would be very zealous to teach Christianity to these poor Illinois savages, of whom most, as is the case with those here, have never heard anything of God. I hope that she will not leave us, there being enough here upon which to exercise her charity. We are not many, and I assure you that we are completely occupied from morning until night. We do not have a minute to ourselves. The time I spend writing to you I take from my night's rest.

Monsieur Perier, our Commandant, had built a prison a few days ago to hold a lady boarder, whom he had himself sent to us because she was separated from her husband. But since this woman began to become bored at the convent and wanted to carry on a secret relationship with a lay person, he had her imprisoned, with the consent of her husband, while trying to ascertain if it was possible to send her back to France. This is the way it is done here.

I told you in one of my previous letters that Monsieur Robert Cavelier, Sieur de LaSalle, native of Rouen, had come with a number of persons also from Rouen, in 1676 and 1685, by the order of King Louis XIV, to this country of Louisiana, to discover the area and to serve as Viceroy of Mississippi. This is all I knew then, but I learned later other circumstances that will please you.

The King was informed in 1675 of this first discovery of the land of the Mississippi by Monsieur de LaSalle and of the esteem that he had earned among the savages, that he was loved by the Illinois, the Hurons, and most other nations along the Mississippi, and that he had found a way to make himself feared and respected by the Iroquois, a nation of the cruelest and most savage in all of America, who eat white people. In 1684, the King appointed him Viceroy of Louisiana, allowed him to raise troops, and gave him four vessels commanded by Captain Beaujeu. The departure was made from LaRochelle about the month of July of the above-mentioned year, 1684.

Monsieur de LaSalle brought with him craftsmen of all trades to make an establishment, and six apostolic missionaries, three ecclesiastics, and three Recollects. The ecclesiastics were Monsieur Jean Cavelier, his brother, Monsieur François de Chefdeville, his relative who had just left St. Sulpice in Paris, and Monsieur de l'Aimanville, who also had come from St. Sulpice. The three Recollects were Fathers Zenoble, Anastase, and Maxime; and a great number of volunteers, who came forward to accompany him, young people carefully chosen, children of native families of Rouen. Among them were Sieurs Cavelier and Crevel du Moranger, his nephews, Henry de Chefdeville, brother of the ecclesiastic, and Desloges, his relatives, Oris, Bihorel, de Clere, Planterose, le Carpentier, Thibault, Tessier le Gras, Minet, de Ville Perdry, Davault, Hurié, Tallon, Gayen, le Noir, L'Archeveque, Liotot, de Marle, Hians, Munier, Joustel, Duhault Frères, des Liettes, le Clerc, Dumensnil, Saget, and many others numbering about 250, including 100 soldiers and their officers, of which Monsieur de la Sablonniere was the lieutenant. Sieur Henry de Chefdeville, eighteen years of age, died of sickness on the vessel after three months' navigation.

He had planned to disembark by the mouth of the Mississippi River, but some miscommunication en route between Monsieur de LaSalle and Sieur de Beaujeu, captain of the vessel of the King, had the effect that they could not find this mouth. And Monsieur de LaSalle was forced to land with the troop about 150 leagues lower on the west side between this river and New Spain, territory of America occupied by the Spanish, in which there are several gold and silver mines, which produce a very considerable profit for the King of Spain every year. Sieur de Beaujeu abandoned Monsieur de LaSalle in this place and returned to France with his vessel.

Monsieur de LaSalle and his troop advanced a great deal upriver then. After having crossed a number of rivers, forests, and plains, they found themselves near the fort of the Illinois, a place that they call today Little Rock, without getting near our area. It is true that at that time there was no city of New Orleans here. It was a deserted and rustic place until the time of the rule of the Duke of Orleans, when they laid the first foundation of this city, and it is for this reason that it is called New Orleans. It did not have the appearance of a city until the year 1723 when they worked as much as they could to find laborers.

Returning to Monsieur de LaSalle: Since this great captain knew how to make himself feared and esteemed by the savages, it seems that everything favored his enterprise. But, in the month of March of 1687, one day when he was ready to send Monsieur Cavelier, his priest brother, to France, to inform the King of the state of the enterprise, he was assassinated in a plot of five of his people because of some kind of jealousy. The crime of Duhault, who dealt him the cruel blow of death, did not remain unpunished because a short time later Hians reproached him for his perfidy and killed him. The four other accomplices have since died unhappily in this country, never having dared return to France.

After the troops lost this brave captain, who alone knew the country, they became equally disoriented, desolate, and dispersed. Monsieur Cavelier, the priest, Sieur Cavelier, his sixteen-year-old nephew, Father Anastase, the Recollect, and Sieurs Joustel and Tessier resolved to return to France. Passing through a village of Acadians, they found there a habitation in which lived a carpenter named Couture, and a cook named Delaunay, both natives of Rouen, whom Monsieur Tonty, then Commander of the Fort of St. Louis in the Illinois Country, had left at the post to guard it. They set off then on the route to Canada, going by way of Fort-Louis, Montreal, and Quebec, where they embarked for the return to France.

The Messieurs Desloges, Oris, Thibault, Le Gras, Liotot, and Carpentier were killed by the savages. The rest of the troops escaped one by one, except Monsieur de Chefdeville, missionary priest, who remained at the same spot, Little Rock, until the month of April 1688 when he went up from the Illinois side toward the Iroquois, where he baptized and converted a great number of souls to God. Then he died in a village in the odor of sanctity to be crowned in heaven in recompense for the ardent zeal that he showed for the salvation of the souls of his poor savages. He was one of the first who had the consolation of opening heaven to the first Christians and saints of this nation.

It is thus that the noble and glorious enterprise of Monsieur de LaSalle failed. Had this evil act not happened, he would have discovered at that time all the country of Mississippi, to which he had given the name of Louisiana. And he would have had there a great number of families who would have come there from France and Canada to establish themselves and to plant the faith. One of those who was in the company of Monsieur de LaSalle at Little Rock was one named Desliettes, who stayed at that place and has only been dead for two years. He reported this in the manner that I have had the honor to tell you. There you have all that I have been able to learn about it.

Your city of Rouen, does it take pride at all, my dear Father, in the honor that it was Monsieur de LaSalle and his company, almost all of them natives of the city, who made the first discovery of the Mississippi? And in Monsieur de Chefdeville, missionary priest, who was one of the first to plant the faith? And finally, today, in the priests and Ursuline nuns of the same city who work at all that is possible at the instruction and the salvation of the souls of these poor savages? This is something to excite your citizens and spur them to the further discovery of other unknown lands, and to take Christianity to them. I do not know if it is for this reason or otherwise that the savages of Louisiana have so much respect for Normans. They regard this province more highly than any of the others and recognize them as capable of succeeding in all their enterprises. If one will speak of the conquests of the Duke of Normandy, the valor of the Normans at the Holy Lands during the Crusades, their conquest of the Kingdom of England and others, they will be further convinced. But, we are not here for that. If they want to know these things, let them be informed by others, or read histories.

I will be curious to know, and I beg you to inform yourself, from which family Monsieur Chefdeville, missionary priest, comes. I heard several times from my grandfather and from our cousin Autin, the Capuchin, that we were related to Monsieur Chefdeville, merchant of Rouen who had, I believe, two sons who were Capuchins, and a daughter who was a Franciscan nun. I believe that it is she whom I have the honor of knowing. She was the Mother Vicar when I left Rouen. We could be of the same family. It will be easy for you to learn from Reverend Father Autin, Superior of the Religious of St. Antoine, if he is still living, or to consult the genealogy that you have of our family. If we are related, it must be on the side of Monsieur Autin or of Monsieur Dumontier, present master of accounts. And if this is as I think, have the goodness to send this information to me by your first letter for I would hope very much to be related to this holy missionary. Being obliged to do more good for his relatives than for others, I would hope to have more of his prayers, which he directs to the Lord in heaven.

You will find enclosed a letter that our very reverend and able Mother Superior writes you. I assure you, my dear Father, that she, as well as all our Mothers, has always thousands and thousands of kindnesses for me. It is impossible for me to express them. I cannot neglect to say that the more I go forward, the more I find myself happy to have heard the voice of the Lord when he called me to a holy vocation. I would hope that all my sisters will do the same. I rejoice to learn that my sister Elizabeth continues to remain at St. Francis with my sister the nun. The more she stays the better she will find it there, for the religious life seems to show nothing to our eyes but thorns. But after having had the experience, the thorns change into roses. In regard to my sister Louison, I pray every day that the Lord will grant me the grace of learning by your first letter of her profession at Val de Grace. That will be a true joy for me.

I had written this letter up to this point, in order, my dear Father, to have it ready to send on the first boat departing for France, but none left. Today is May 8, 1728. Having learned that one is ready to sail I finish it now. I have nothing new to tell you, only that I have had some fever for several days. Yesterday, to get over it, I took an emetic, the medicine one ordinarily takes in this country.

Our Reverend Mother and dear Superior remains indisposed. Our other Mothers are perfectly well. They all asked me to send you their regards.

We got rid of that woman of whom I wrote you, who was a prisoner in our house. A counselor of the country let it slip that he would be willing to have her in his home. Monsieur Perier, our Commandant, had her conducted to his house, and put her under his care.

I pray to the Lord every day to keep all of you in perfect health, and I am, from the bottom of my heart, very respectfully,

My dear Father,

Your very humble and very obedient daughter and servant,

Hachard of St. Stanislaus

FIG. 1. A fully professed Ursuline choir nun.
Ancienne Ursuline Congregée en Provence.

From Pierre Hélyot, *Histoire des ordres monastiques religieux et militaires, et des congregations seculieres de l'un & l'autre sexe, qui ont été établies jusque' à présent,* vol 4 (Paris: Gosselin, 1715). General Research Division, New York Public Library, Astor, Lenox and Tilden Foundations. Used by permission.

FIG. 2. This sketch shows the port in Saint Domingue, which Hachard called *Caille St. Louis*. Notice the island fort, to which Hachard refers. *Les Cayes.*

From Pierre Caillot, "Relation du Voyage de la Louisianne ou Nouvelle France fait par Sr. Caillot en l'Annee 1730." Watercolor. Historic New Orleans Collection. Used by permission.

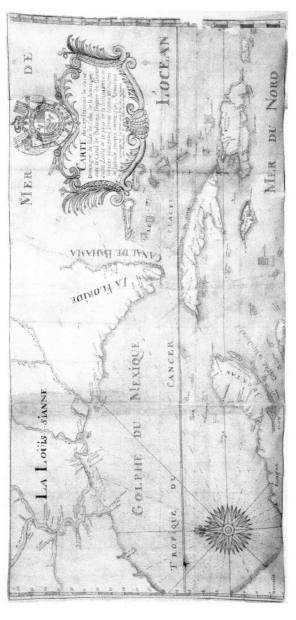

FIG. 3. *Map of Cap Francois of Saint Domingue . . . and Louisiana and adjacent islands*, circa 1729. From Dumont de Montigny, *Memoire de Lxx Dxx Officiere Ingenieur*.

Courtesy Edward E. Ayer Collection, Newberry Library.

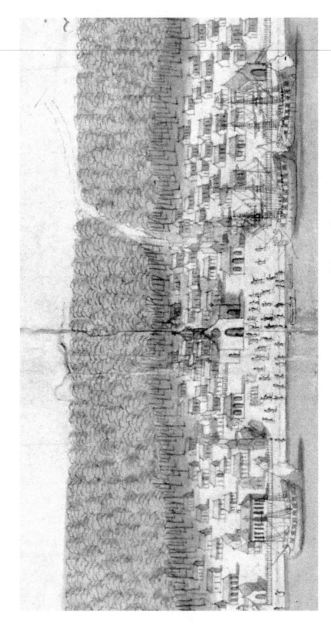

FIG. 4. Jean-Pierre Lassus, *Veüe et Perspective de la Nouvelle Orléans*, 1726.
Courtesy Centre des Archives d'Outre-Mer, Aix en Provence, France, FR CAOM 04DFC71A.

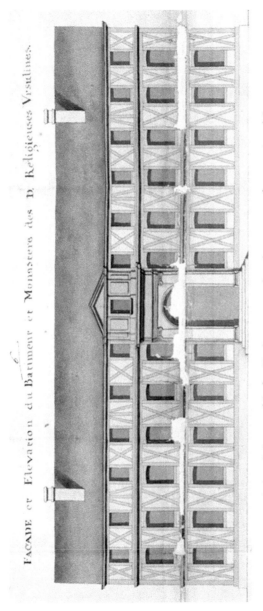

FAÇADE et Élévation du Bâtiment et Monastere des D. Religieuses Ursulines.

FIG. 5. Architect's drawing of the first Ursuline convent, where the procession of 1734 terminated. Ignace-François Broutin, *Façade et élévation du Bâtiment et Monastère des D. Religieuses Ursulines. Coupe profil du Bâtiment et Monnastère des Dames Ursulines de cette ville à la Nlle Orléans le 14 janvier 1732.*

Courtesy Centre des Archives d'Outre-Mer, Aix en Provence, France, FR CAOM F3/290/6

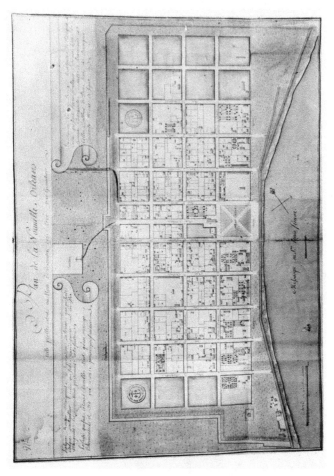

FIG. 6. The Ursuline property is at the extreme lower right of the plan. The key to the map notes the "House which they are constructing for the Ursulines. They are due to have the two squares marked R for their enclosure." Gonichon, *Plan de la Nouvelle Orléans telle qu'elle estoit au mois de dexembre 1731 levé par Gonichon*, FR CAOM 04DFC898B.

Courtesy Centre des Archives d'Outre-Mer, Aix en Provence, France, FR CAOM 04DFC898B.

PART 2

OBITUARY LETTERS

INTRODUCTION

The obituary letter written by the mother superior at the time of each nun's death is, in most cases, the only biographical information we have about the individuals who entered religious life at the New Orleans Ursuline convent. These documents are especially illuminating because they often describe the family background and youth of a sister, as well as her religious career. Technically speaking, the Ursulines shed their worldly identities when they professed as nuns and took their final vows, in effect dying to the outside world and to their families. Part of the ceremony of profession actually included draping a funeral pall over the new nun as she prostrated herself before the altar. The religious ideal also called for nuns to relinquish their individual identities as they assumed their place in the corporate body of their community of sisters. The obituary letters that follow, however, show that some traces of a nun's prior life survived her passage into the convent enclosure, and that her individuality was not wholly subsumed into a faceless mass of women.[1]

The most obvious evidence of continuity between a sister's past and present ways of life was her name. When a young woman was clothed with the habit of a religious order upon entering the novitiate, she was given a "name in religion." Ursulines in colonial New Orleans addressed one another by their religious names, as did their students, but their family names were never permanently retired. In correspondence with the outside world, and when individual nuns were mentioned in documents produced both inside and outside the convent, their family names were commonly combined with their religious names. Thus the founding mother superior of the New Orleans convent, born Marie Tranchepain, is referred to in her obituary letter as "Reverend Mother Marie Tranchepain called St. Augustin."

Descriptions of sisters as children and young women are often included in the obituaries, further blurring the line between their secular and religious lives. A young girl's piety, her struggle to follow her religious vocation, and even her parents' religiosity were all common elements in obituary letters. The visibility of such details was clearly deemed to be important to

1. Details about Ursuline profession and the relationship between pre- and post-convent life are based on *Règlemens des religieuses Ursulines de la congrégation de Paris* (Paris: Chez Louis Josse, 1705).

There is a large body of scholarship on the emergence of individualism in the early modern period, much of it growing out of Norbert Elias, *The Civilizing Process: Sociogenetic and Psychogenetic Investigations,* trans. Edmund Jephcott (Oxford: Oxford University Press, 1994).

the construction of a full spiritual biography, even as convents enforced the invisibility to the outside world of the details of a sister's life after she professed her final vows.

One of the tenets of the Ursulines' educational philosophy was to recognize the individuality of each student who came under their charge and to teach her in a way that encouraged the achievement of certain intellectual and religious standards without compromising the distinctiveness of the student's talents and temperament. This outlook may well reflect a general movement toward individualism that has been identified by historians as a feature of the early modern period. In any event, the obituary notices of the New Orleans Ursulines testify to their attentiveness to the diversity of gifts among their sisters. In them we meet women characterized by abject humility, dangerous enthusiasm, iron resolve, and sweet submissiveness. Each was eulogized for her unique array of qualities, and we understand by reading these notices that there was no single ideal to guide an Ursuline as she sought to perfect herself in religious life in the strange new setting that was Louisiana. The Ursuline community drew on the power of its corporate identity and material resources to manage the challenges that it encountered in Louisiana, yet its success also depended on the ability of each nun to deploy her individuality to the convent's best advantage in the face of unforeseen and unfamiliar circumstances. Each of the founding sisters contributed, in her own way, to a manifestation of her order that was unparalleled in previous incarnations of the Company of St. Ursula in France and Canada, helping to create a uniquely American institution.

"Circular Letters of deceased Nuns in this new
monastery of New Orleans, province of Louisiana."

*On the 6 of July 1728 our very dear sister Madeleine
Mahieu of St. Francis Xavier, professed of Le
Havre in the province of Normandy, died.*

My very Reverend Mothers,

It is with eyes brimming with tears and a heart seized with
sorrow that I address you to solicit the sympathy of our order
for my dear sister Madeleine Mahieu called St. Francis Xavier,
whom we have just lost. I cannot detail for you the virtues that
she practiced during her youth, not having had the good fortune to know her before she joined us to make our foundation.
Her humility left her hidden even to herself. We know only
that she was allowed to enter with difficulty, as we were made
aware that her mother opposed her entering religion and this
dear girl did not succeed in having the good fortune such that
she could aspire to do so until the death of this lady. Then, finding herself free to execute her pious design and embracing the
religious life with all the dispositions that one could wish for
in a novice to make a perfect nun, she profited so well from the
instructions that she received in her novitiate that she attracted
the loving regard of her divine spouse, who filled her with His
spirit and gave her the desire to consecrate herself anew to Him
for the mission to Louisiana, some ten years before it was even
thought to make an establishment of our order there, and at a

time when such a plan seemed impossible.[2] She addressed St.
Francis Xavier to obtain this grace. Her wishes and desires ever
redoubling as the time for the execution of the act approached,
she hoped against all hope that the Lord, in his mercy, would
in the end grant her prayers. She was of this disposition when
she learned that the Reverend Father de Beaubois, Superior
General of the missions in this country, was coming to Paris
to arrange an establishment of Ursulines at New Orleans and
that for that purpose he had cast his eyes on three nuns of the
Community of Rouen. She wrote them with all the ardor that
such a vocation can inspire, and she easily obtained a favorable
response from Reverend Father de Beaubois and the three nuns
already chosen. But it was not so easy to obtain the consent of
her community, and especially of the dignified mother superior
who had authority over it, who, being acquainted with the solid
virtue of this sister, was unable to consent to losing her. She,
on her side, made no little sacrifice in leaving this dear Mother,
whom she loved perfectly in Jesus Christ. But in the end, the
power of grace enabled her to triumph with a pure heart, and
with a metaphysical act she fulfilled God's plans for her. The
Reverend Mother Superior did all that she could to keep a
treasure that she knew to be priceless. She wrote about this to
Reverend Father de Beaubois and the nuns to keep them from
accepting Sister St. Xavier, citing the frailty of her constitution.
But the prayers, perseverance, and fervor of that sister disarmed
the Superior who consented in the end to the will of God. Now
nothing remained except requesting her obedience from Mon-

---

2. When a woman took her solemn vows as a nun, she symbolically became
the bride of Christ, hence references to a nun's divine spouse.

signor Archbishop of Rouen, but he refused it because he was strongly opposed to this enterprise.[3] We were obliged to address ourselves to his Eminence the Cardinal de Fleury, minister of State. While we were employing earthly influence, our dear sister acted with much better efficiency, through the Almighty, through prayers and tears. We were, however, obliged to leave for Lorient, and despite ourselves we left this fervent missionary behind, in uncertainty about whether she would be able to rejoin us. Finally, Our Lord having received enough proof, she received her obedience and left immediately to meet us, at the Ursulines of Hennebont, accompanied by a young nun of Elboeuf and a postulant. Everywhere we stopped this excellent sister edified everyone; but it was principally at the house of our Reverend Mothers the Ursulines of the Rue St. Jacques in Paris, where they made a visit of six weeks, that one came to know her virtue by the proofs that she gave that drew her to the attention and the probity of the Reverend Mother de Bruvel called St. Amand, of the first monastery of our order. This Reverend Mother, in whom good taste and merit are known, honored her with her friendship. She continued her journey in the same

3. AC, C13A, 10:319–319v; Elizabeth Rapley, *A Social History of the Cloister: Daily Life in the Teaching Monasteries of the Old Regime* (Montreal: McGill-Queen's University Press, 2001), 29–48. The approval of an ecclesiastical superior with jurisdiction over their convent, usually the bishop of the diocese, was required both for a woman to enter a convent and for a vowed nun to leave one convent for another. This approval was called an obedience. The archbishop of Rouen opposed the Louisiana mission until he received assurances that the Crown would guarantee the nuns' support in the event of the financial failure of the Company of the Indies. French convents had been in a precarious financial position for decades, and the prelate wanted to be certain that the nuns would not return to their original convents in France, further burdening them.

manner, everywhere showing the same virtues. Finally, she arrived at Hennebont, and there we began to know her by the
traits of the most delicate virtue that one is able to report. She
did not change at all during the voyage, and five months of a
difficult navigation did not cause any alternation in her even
temperament. All these good qualities that she possessed led to
naming her Mother Mistress of the three novices we had. Her
humility led her to oppose this choice, but obedience prevailed.
She submitted to her superiors as she had to her God. I also
put her in charge of our linen; she acquitted herself of that task
with a fervor that frequently obliged me to restrain her, lest
she act beyond her limits. She asked me to allow her to care
for the instruction of the savagesses and negresses, but having engaged another, I accorded her the instruction of the day
students. She did so with delight and never was more content
than when she saw them grow in number. The more ignorant
they were the more she was attached to them. If I did not fear
exceeding the limits of this account I would dwell on her other
virtues, especially her obedience, which she carried to perfec-
tion. She had no trouble relinquishing her own judgment; she
had only to have the slightest sign. Her concern for herself was
equally sincere, she was indignant at the least little attention
to herself. She could not admire the charity of others enough.
Her mortification was without equal; she ate everything indif-
ferently without remarking what she found good or bad. She
joined to these virtues a lovable simplicity that made her gay
without being silly. She had a good spirit capable of carrying
out everything for the glory of God and the salvation of souls
without taking anything for herself.

She was sick but eight days with a fever that did not seem considerable until the eve of her death, when she fell unconscious. After a bleeding at the foot, she fell into a weakened state from which she was unable to recover. We then learned that her illness was an abscess in her head. During her agony, our Reverend Father Superior administered the holy oils to her, after which she rendered her spirit.[4] There was nothing but cries and sobs in our house, as much on the part of our boarding students as the orphans, the day students, and our slaves. She was loved generally by all. All the city took part in our loss and our sorrow. Finally, for my part, my heart is penetrated by the most piercing sadness. I ask you to pray to our Lord, Reverend Mother, to remain at her side and to send us some holy and

4. The administration of holy oils to which the eulogist refers is the sacrament of extreme unction, the fourth step in a series of six actions known as the last rites, administered when death seems imminent. Not all of the obituaries chronicle the full series, but the sequence is provided here for reference.

The Catholic Church recognizes seven sacraments: baptism, the Eucharist or Holy Communion, absolution, confirmation, marriage, holy orders, and extreme unction. The last rites include the three sacraments of the Eucharist, absolution, and extreme unction. They begin with confession and the sacrament of absolution, which must be administered by a priest. After confession, the moribund person receives the sacrament of the Eucharist, known in this circumstance as the *viaticum*. The administration of extreme unction follows the viaticum. Extreme unction was generally not given more than once during the same illness, but if a person seemed to come to a death crisis and then rebound, it might be administered more than once. Following extreme unction, the priest confers the apostolic benediction, commonly known as the last blessing. As the final death agony approaches, the priest pronounces the recommendation of a departing soul. Finally, as the person is about to expire, those at the deathbed recite, on behalf of the dying person, a variety of traditional prayers such as "Into thy hands, Lord, I commend my spirit"; "O Lord, Jesus Christ, receive my spirit"; "Holy Mary, pray for me"; and "Mary mother of grace, mother of mercy, do thou protect me from the enemy and receive me at the hour of my death."

capable person to take her place, for we are in need, not being of sufficient number for the work that we have to do.

I have the honor to hold you in perfect consideration and much respect,

My very Reverend Mother,

Your very humble and very obedient servant,

Sister Marie Tranchepain of St. Augustine

Superior

The 14th of August 1731 our dear mother Marguerite Judde died. She was professed of the community of Rouen. She edified us abundantly by her actions and her virtues, particularly her work for the salvation of souls, her character and her humility, as will be seen by what follows.

My dear Reverend Mother,

It is with great sadness and a heart heavy with regret that I call upon your goodness to obtain the prayers of our holy order in favor of our dear mother Marguerite Judde of St. Jean the Evangelist. She was a member of the community of Ursulines of Rouen, from which her zeal for the love of God and the salvation of souls made her leave to come to this mission in New Orleans, capital of the province of Louisiana to begin a new establishment. I am unable to express the loss we feel in the death of this dear person. Her virtue and her merit made her esteemed and loved by everyone who knew her, both inside and outside the convent. She had such a strong vocation to work for the salvation of souls that as soon as she knew about the establishment of Ursulines here, she felt herself fortunate to discover an occasion to sacrifice herself one more time, afresh, for her heavenly spouse. But this sacrifice of herself was not the only thing that she did. Her family of brothers and sisters, which lived in the same city as she did and by whom she was tenderly loved, strongly opposed her plan. But our dear mother, thinking of herself only as a victim consecrated to the pure glory of God, remained true to the voice that called her, thus all the reasons that her parents put before her to deter her only served to amplify her generosity and her courage. Not once in our arduous five-month crossing did she complain about what she was suffering. No sooner had we arrived here than she began to demonstrate her zeal for the instruction of the slaves. She was named assistant, and she fulfilled this charge until the end of her life to the edification of all. She had all the virtues that one could wish for in a good nun, particularly her zeal for regularity. She was always the first at all observances and she wanted to be in charge of waking the community, and although she was already quite old and had need of her night's rest, she always continued this task. Her charity towards her sisters was universal, tending to all their needs up to the point where she would give all that she had. The holy Ursuline mothers of Rouen should render homage particularly for, despite the poverty of the house, all the pensions and presents that parents gave her in abundance were used to relieve the suffering and the sick, but particularly the latter who were always the objects of her attentions. This care and capacity was no less apparent in her charge as treasurer which she held for two years; she spared herself nothing for the good of the community. She was provident and organized in her accounts, such that she left the affairs of the house in good order. It would take too long to recount here in detail all the virtues of this dear mother, but certainly I cannot remain silent on the delicacy of her conscience. She declared a little before her death that she had never deliberately caused pain to anyone. She had a good and compassionate heart and was very hardworking and wanted always to spare others. Mortification seemed to be one of her favorite virtues because she mortified herself without ever making it seem anything out of the ordinary. She was no less edifying, during her last illness, by her submission, wanting what we wanted and only what we wanted, and always, no matter what, wanting to be governed like a child, never showing any impatience. In the end, an illness of six weeks ended this happy life.

She had nothing at first but two rather strong attacks of fever, which decreased and nearly left her well. But there remained a great headache which made her lose her sense of the beginning of her illness in such a way that she could not see how the fever was increasing. Soon she demanded confession and she made a general confession and had the good fortune to receive her last communion and extreme unction. Two days later and having said all the prayers, it was time to administer the last rites.[5] Soon she fell into a kind of lethargy. She revived a bit the day before her death and told us again of the good feelings that God was giving her, especially those of resignation, desire, and confidence.

5. See note 4 above for a description of the last rites.

My very Reverend Mother,
Your very humble and very obedient servant
Sister Marie Tranchepain, Superior

The fifth of September 1733 our dear sister Marguerite Talaon
of St. Therese, nun professed of the community of Ploermel
in Brittany, died and was interred the sixth of this month.
She edified us greatly by her virtue, particularly her great
submission to obedience as you shall see by what follows.

My very Reverend Mother,

If my sadness were able to be expressed it would comfort me to tell you everything that my heart embraces regarding the new complaint that it has just received by virtue of the loss that our community has just experienced of our very dear and very loveable sister St. Therese. In the world her name was Marguerite Talaon and she was the daughter of a highly esteemed lawyer in Brittany and was closely related to the most distinguished families of this great province. She was born in Ploermel and it was there that she consecrated to God that which she had. Attaining the necessary age, she chose the Ursulines not only because she had sucked the milk of piety in their boarding school, but even more because she had remarked in this holy house a fervor and a regularity that made her regard it as a reassuring aide against the dangers of the world. She did not mislead herself in this, for although we know nearly nothing of her novitiate, I am able to tell that she learned true and solid virtue, which does not consist so much in exterior demonstrations as in the fidelity to battle against herself. It was this holy and constant practice that was the source of an infinity of sacrifices that she made to our Lord, the mere memory of which made her surmount all the difficulties of life and made her appear a little imperious. She had a good heart, just, and sincere, an expansive and enlightened spirit, loving to oblige everyone, and without reservation for her friends, whose interests were dearer to her than her own. But God, who wanted to possess her uniquely, made her sense in good time the necessity of her loving nothing but Him and to detach herself from that which she held most dear in the world, which was an only brother and a sister-in-law, whom she loved tenderly and who loved her equally. Though this love seemed to her innocent she nevertheless carried a secret reproach from our Lord, which made her finally resolve to break the ties that impeded her from intimately serving her spouse. This was the thing that was at the root of her vocation for the missions, to which she promised God she would consecrate herself when he gave her the occasion. After this promise she became calmer, imagining herself perhaps to have settled things. But our Lord soon made her aware that he was not content with this willingness and that he wanted the act, and his providence disposed everything to that end. She learned that there were Ursulines at Hennebont who were nuns from Rouen who were waiting to embark to go to make an establishment in Louisiana. Thus, true to the grace within, despite natural repugnance, she wrote to me with fervor to obtain leave to join with us, and God, who had inspired this thought, gave me at the same time a strong inclination to prefer a greater number of others who sought to join us. I did not hesitate to invite her. Her plan was soon discovered and her brother, having spoken against it, spared nothing to break her resolve—affection, tears, reproaches, and threats—all were employed to keep her. But if she had combat outside, the war inside was no less painful. Her community, which loved her and which held her infinitely dear, opposed all its forces to her plan. Her superior also, although full of zeal and virtue, was unable to resign herself to the loss. The delicacy of her constitution appeared an insurmountable pretext. They consulted doctors who declared that she could never travel more than fifty leagues by sea. This made them redouble all their oppositions, but her great courage allowed her to surmount them all. She came finally to join us and undertook without fear a voyage of 2500 leagues, imperiling a life that wanted nothing but to love God. It was by means of these sentiments that she prevailed without trembling several times at the point of peril, without having the least appearance of fear. "What does it matter," she said to me, "to die here? Allow me to die doing the will of God who has asked this of me. All that He wants of me shall be. I abandon myself to His providence." This fundamental disposition endured with her always. When she deviated a little she soon returned. She was employed in all occupations, even the most difficult and despite her weak health I always found her prepared for anything. Finally God called her to be our dear mother treasurer. I could not have better placed the direction of temporal affairs than in the hands of our dear sister, who had, we noticed, much talent for this and whose penetration of spirit aided her in doing everything well. I followed this counsel and we find ourselves well situated. Nothing seemed difficult for her and that which would upset another was never a trouble for her, she always finding new means of overcoming difficulties and to improve the House without compromising her conscience, in a country where one finds this a challenge. But we did not profit for long of this rare talent. It was on the sixteenth of May that she was taken with a flux that lasted for two or three months, without ever saying anything, and it was only by her great lack of appetite that one realized that she was ill and this obliged her to declare her illness.[6] They consulted the doctor, who administered one after the other all the proper remedies, but all seemed to do nothing but worsen her illness. Finally, a change of air was attempted but all was useless and the weakness of her body finally succumbed entirely and the fever took her. We despaired of her life. She was not at all alarmed. The long duration of her illness had made her detached from everything. Accomplishing the will of God was her sole desire and she spoke of her impending death like a thing that did not interest her at all. She prayed of me only that I not abandon her in her extremity and to speak to her of nothing but of God. The Reverend Father Vitry, missionary of the Company of Jesus recently arrived from France, did as she asked to help, to the degree he could. This holy father, full of virtue and of zeal, as well as merit, perfectly acquitted this sad commission

6. A flux is a discharge from an organ or cavity of the body, most commonly involving blood and/or feces. It is almost impossible to determine what the underlying condition or disease was when reference is made to a flux, and only occasionally is the source of the flux mentioned, as it was in the case of Sister Cécile of the Angels. See page 115 and note 10 below.

and made the end as good as it could be, serving as the agent of edifying dispositions in the midst of which she received the holy *viaticum* with joy and a perfect peacefulness. Two days later she seemed very ill. It was judged appropriate to give her extreme unction, which she received while still conscious, but she did not speak again, and a moment afterwards she entered into a sweet agony which lasted no more than a quarter of an hour, after which she expired, the fifth of September 1733, like a child and without anyone being aware of her last breath. She was aged about thirty-two years. Her face, which the illness had greatly changed, soon retook its natural air with a sweetness that one could not help but admire. In place of a certain fear that the appearance of a dead person inspires, one should find this. All the city was aware of her death and all of the most important people were at her burial. Most wept, for without disguising the truth, she showed each the secret of being loved. Her great attraction was her love for and confidence in our Lord and his holy mother, given with perfect obedience. My reverend mother, it will be to you to judge the greatness of my pain, especially for a community which has barely begun and which is already so small in number, for now we are reduced to eight, of whom many are in poor health.

The eleventh of November 1733 died our Reverend Mother Marie Tranchepain of St. Augustine, while holding the charge of superior, after having given us proofs of a consummate virtue in all that one could wish in a perfect nun and worthy superior, as one shall see before long in what follows.

This letter will inform you, my Reverend Mother, of the very great loss which this house has just had of our Reverend Mother Marie Tranchepain called St. Augustine, the first and worthy superior. The extent of our affliction is magnified by the benefit that we had in possessing a daughter of such rare merit and so filled with all of the eminent qualities desirable for a good governor and all that might render her an object of respect, even to those persons least touched by virtue. Her approach was gracious and her manner the most ingratiating in the world. Her spirit was lively and penetrating, her conversation lively but always seasoned adroitly with matters of God, whom she found the means to please and to edify. It was by this that she found means to compensate herself for the worry that was caused her by the frequent commerce that she was obliged to have with secular persons, which would have been unbearable to her if she had not been able to obtain profit for the health of the community. The sweetest pleasure that she savored was to be alone for conversation with God, whose presence she never lost, even in the middle of the most dissipated occupations. Her devotion towards our Lord and his holy mother was the most tender and solid. One was not able to see how touching this was until we found this in her papers after her death.

Raised in the great world and in the way of the reformed Protestant religion, God made his conquest by his strokes of grace, achieving a miracle. Our reverend mother remained true to it. She followed all the movements exactly and surmounted generally the obstacles that were opposed to her conversion, which had appeared invincible to everyone but her. She was raised by her parents, who loved her tenderly and to whom she was strongly attached, and was led to our Ursulines of Rouen where she made her abjuration into the hands of Monsieur l'Abbe de Gapanuille, grand vicar of Monsignor the Archbishop. Then, touched by God and edified by the virtues of this holy community, she determined to embrace our holy institute in this house. She made her entry into the novitiate in 1699 with extraordinary fervor. In these early times, she sensed a singular attraction for the missions. Our Lord Jesus Christ and his holy mother made her know that she had much to suffer before going there and when she arrived there. All that simply increased her zeal, seeming to the contrary to render her more lively and more ardent. This she left us in her writings on the disposition of her heart, so admirable and revealing well the greatness of her courage, which she showed by its effects, that is to say with a generosity uncommon in the face of the difficulties, pain, and dismay that are inseparable from the founding of an establishment. Although our reverend mother had made several attempts to fulfill the visions that she had, she was unable to doubt that providence was with her. God made known to her that a Jesuit whom she did not know and who did not know her who was passing through France was he who would become her guide to conduct her to a strange land where He wanted her to serve by founding an establishment of the nuns of her order. The Jesuit was the Reverend Father de Beaubois, who was obliged to make a voyage to France for the affairs of his mission and who had a plan to work to establish a community of Ursulines in New Orleans. He happily came to the culmination of his plan in 1726, having proposed to the governors of the Company of the Indies the foundation of a hospital of which the community would be in charge. This reverend father having become aware of the zeal that consumed our dear mother wrote to her the ideas that he had for her. I do not need to tell you, my Reverend Mother, what transports of joy beset our fervent missionary at the moment when she saw her vows fulfilled, heightened by what she had suffered to execute her plans for so many years. Her virtue, her courage and her ability to cultivate the spirit helped her to surmount the obstacles.

After having concluded our treaty of foundation with the directors of the Company of the Indies, on which Louisiana depended, she then left Paris with our dear Sisters Judde and Boulenger to go to Lorient, where, after three months' sojourn she embarked a company of eleven professed nuns, one novice, and two postulants destined to be converse sisters.[7]

The crossing was long and difficult. Many times they found themselves in great danger. The captain of the ship did not treat them well, one is able to say, refusing them even the necessities of life. His refusals were accompanied by methods so brutal that they seemed insupportable to everyone except our dear Mother. But her patience and that of her daughters did not falter for one moment. They received everything with politesse and calmness. Her example and her encouraging conversation brought them at last to New Orleans at the beginning of Au-

---

7. This count of the number of founding sisters in incorrect. There were eight fully professed choir nuns, one novice choir nun, two converse sisters, and a postulant, for a total of twelve. See note 2, part 1.

gust. From that day and until the day of her death God tried
her by crosses and obvious difficulties that succeeded one after
the other, which she bore with an equanimity of spirit that
brought her the admiration of everyone who witnessed it. For
it came to pass that those same ones who contributed to the
foundation with the best intentions of the world were those
who tried her patience, bringing things to the point of entirely
destroying this work which she had been given by God.[8] But
the confidence that she had in His goodness upheld her.

The humility of our dear mother hid the great talents that
she received to direct others. She carried on neither the conduct
of her monastery nor of herself without also consulting with
those in whom she had confidence. It was not by obedience that
she remained for so long charged with the office of superior, but
because it was so difficult to find a sister who had more merit
and capacity than she had.

She was attacked on the feast day of St. Ursula, 1733, with
a violent stomach colic. Her fever did not abate at all; she of-
ficiated as ordinarily although she continued to have attacks of
this illness. She went to bed at night and despite the high fever

8. It is not clear who is meant here. Tranchepain's difficulties in the early years
of the mission were legion. The eulogist may be referring to officers of the Company
of the Indies, to the Jesuits, or to inhabitants of New Orleans who took a special
interest in the convent. The Company of the Indies, including its spiritual director,
Abbé Raguet, seems the most likely candidate: it failed to build the nuns' convent in
good time, insisted in 1729 on their taking on a large number of orphans who strained
their resources, tried to impose a clerical superior of its choosing on the women, and
refused to increase financial assistance to them. At one point in 1728, Tranchepain
threatened to take the entire New Orleans Ursuline community to Cap Français in
Saint Domingue. See Heaney, *Century of Pioneering*, 72–91.

that she had all night, she rose the next day and was on her feet throughout the day. Finally on the twenty-fourth, the illness was declared so serious that on the twenty-sixth she appeared in peril. Several doctors who visited her assured us to the contrary, but she requested the holy *viaticum,* persuaded that she was dying. She received it with the most tender of pious sentiments. Her illness seemed to diminish a little; we had hope that she would be able to recover. It was nonetheless necessary to curb the desire which burned within her to see God and to be united with him. She was distressed when told that she was not departing the world, and seized by a great sadness. Her illness and a high fever continued over eighteen days. She bore this suffering with holy patience. She suffered from a flux.

The eighteenth day of her illness, after receiving the holy *viaticum* for the second time, she asked to receive the sacrament of extreme unction, which was administered to her by the Reverend Father de Beaubois, whom Father Raphael, Capuchin, at that time grand vicar of the Archbishop of Quebec, had permitted to attend to her, although forbidden by the unjust prohibition which had been given by this prelate, which was not one of the least of the crosses of our dear Mother. She received her last sacraments with all the marks of the most vital piety. Finally, on the eleventh of November of this year, 1733, she rendered her beautiful soul to God at half past three in the morning. One may say of her that she did not lose the presence of God during the entire course of her illness, having his spirit always with her up to the last instant and always thinking of Heaven. We are persuaded that she will not be delayed in reaching her goal.

Sister Cécile called of the Angels, deceased in 1742 at the
age of forty-five years, the eleventh of December.[9]

This letter will advise you, my Reverend Mother, of the loss that has just occurred of our dear sister Cécile called of the Angels, Ursuline of Elboeuf. From her entry into religious life she had an ardent desire to consecrate herself to the missions, and she addressed herself for that purpose to St. Joseph, toward whom she had a tender devotion, inventing every day new ways to honor him. She promised to this great saint that if he obtained for her the realization of her request, she would change her name to that of St. Joseph. Her prayers were granted: the Reverend Father de Beaubois agreed for her to join with the other Ursulines who were leaving for America. She promptly fell grievously ill and suffered greatly during the five months of the crossing, but she then miraculously recovered and, although she never enjoyed perfect health, she undertook great works for the good of the House. She was charged with teaching our class of day students and with catechizing black men and women. She had a boundless zeal for these tasks, which, on several occasions, caused her superiors to forbid her this work in order to moderate her activities. One saw with consolation that she made much progress in all these diverse tasks and one could

9. The obituary letter for Cécile des Angels begins in the middle of p. 211 of the original "Lettres circulaires." The bottom half of this page is very badly damaged, rendering much of the original letter illegible. The translation here uses what is left of the original and fills in gaps with a nineteenth-century manuscript copy of the early letters.

say that she contributed well to the establishment of piety in families, as much the whites as the blacks. There were a number for whom she procured by her instruction the good fortune to receive the sacraments of baptism and of the Eucharist, which they approached with edification having been, by her care and upheld by the grace of God, rid of their libertine ways. Thus these good people showed their feelings upon her death in a manner that was most touching and full of gratitude. These poor black women added to their tears and sorrow the care to pray to God for her, forcing the one who took her place to receive considerable sums, in view of their limited means, to say masses for the repose of her soul. They said that they could not do enough for her.

She died, one would say, weapons at hand, having hidden her illness, which was a congestion of the chest, for more than fifteen days without ever reducing her usual exertions.[10] Finally, the last day of November after having attended the holy sacrifice of the Mass and made her confession in chapter, she took to her bed. The doctor came two hours later and was greatly surprised to find her so grievously ill. All the remedies were unable to stop the illness, which had made too much progress. She preserved all the presence of spirit necessary to make holy use of her time. She performed the most touching acts of religion. Father Doutreleau, Jesuit, attended her with the most edified charity and assiduousness, sparing nothing day and night. Fi-

10. I have translated the original *fluxion de poitrine* as "congestion of the chest," a symptom that may have marked the end stages of tuberculosis or pneumonia. See note 6 above for a discussion of the term *flux*.

nally, on the eleventh of December, she rendered her soul at two o'clock in the morning, aged forty-five years and twenty-one and a half years in profession.

Whatever virtues our dear sister showed us during the course of her life of holy missionary work, we do not ask you the sufferance of our order to pursue canonization for this dear departed one. God, who comes with torch in hand to visit Jerusalem and to judge us, accords a small part to her who had the honor to be in the holy calling of Jesus.

Your very humble and obedient servant,
Sister St. Pierre, Superior

My dear Mother,

God visits us with an affliction all the more acute for its having been completely unforeseen: it is the death of our dear sister Marie Madeleine Hachard called St. Stanislaus.[11]

This dear sister was the daughter of Monsieur Hachard, procurer in the Chamber of Accounts at Rouen, distinguished by his honesty. Her mother, who possessed a large allotment of piety, neglected nothing to provide the most Christian education to the seven children whom the Lord gave her, of whom the greater number are consecrated to Him by the holy vows of religion.

She whom we mourn was the youngest. During her child-

11. "Ursuline Annals I," Ursuline Convent of New Orleans Archives, 264–65. Hachard's obituary letter does not give the date of her death, but it is recorded in the convent annals as August 9, 1760.

hood, one noticed in her such judgment and devotion that she was found capable of making her first communion at the age of ten. On approaching the holy table her tender piety increased anew, such that she frequently arose in the night to pray. At the age of eighteen years her parents wanted to betroth her in marriage. An advantageous match having been presented, she refused it. God, who had taken possession of her heart wanted her in holy orders. She presented herself to the Sisters of St. Francis at the age of twenty years and postulated herself before their grille according to the custom of this order, but her confessor deterred her from this, assuring her that it was not what God wanted of her. Some time afterwards, having heard that there were plans for an establishment of religious of our order in New Orleans in the Province of Louisiana and that the mothers of our convent of Rouen had been chosen to found it, she was inspired to propose herself to them and prayed of them to permit her to share with them the difficult labors which are inseparable from a new foundation. Such an undertaking by a young person merited serious examination of her character and her talents. After three months, during which they neglected nothing in order to know her well, she was received with inexpressible joy. It cost her many tears to obtain the consent of her family, who, opposing such a remote project, made it difficult for her to go. In the end, religion, which filled her mother and father, overcame the ties of blood. She left with our foundresses, making a vow to imitate their virtues.

She performed all the jobs of this house with admirable exactitude and tirelessness. She loved to oblige everyone without exception. Grace raised in her all her good qualities by a tender devotion to Jesus and the holy sacrament of the altar, which she had the good fortune to receive no less than four times each week. Her attraction to poverty made her deny the most necessary things. Her extreme regularity of religious observance made her able to earn the just title, "living Rule of the house."

When death came for her she was employed with our boarding students. She spent the ninth of August with them without any sign of the coming disaster. The next day, not having seen her at Mass, we knew that she was ill, and went to her cell. There we found her dead in her bed. But this did not worry me, because she prepared herself every day by thinking of her death.[12] She fulfilled the various functions with which she was charged and repaired the faults we made, relieving and replacing those whom age and infirmity rendered unable to work. May you be inclined towards her that she may rest in the sacred heart of Jesus.

My very Reverend Mother,
Your very humble and very obedient servant,
Sister Marie of St. Therese of Jesus, Superior

12. The manuscript becomes almost totally illegible from this point to the end of the letter. The closing lines are the translator's best attempt at rendering the sense of the biographer's sentiments from the words that can be made out.

PART 3

PROCESSION ACCOUNT

INTRODUCTION

The account of a procession planned and carried out by the New Orleans Ursulines in 1734 acquaints us with an unusual example of women's participation in civic life before the emergence of the modern public sphere and electoral politics. Students of American women's history are well acquainted with the ways post-Revolutionary women eluded the ideological confines of the private domestic sphere that had been conjured for them by using it as a base from which to launch benevolent and reformist campaigns that were undeniably public in their impact. In this way women invaded the public sphere of civic responsibility and action without benefit of the vote. Yet theirs was a backdoor entrance onto the public stage. The ideology of republican citizenship equated the voting male citizenry with the public and in so doing formally excluded women from the public sphere. Only when women gained the vote in the early twentieth century did they become full citizens with an unlimited range of authorized action in civil society.[1]

Rank, rather than gender, governed the rules of engagement in the public arena prior to the birth of male republican citizenries in the wake of the American and French revolutions. The power to make political decisions in both early modern Europe and the New World colonies resided with a small number of elite men. The representational governmental bodies that did exist were limited in their powers and were elected only by those who held significant property. The significant majority of early modern people—men and women—who were without authority to make political decisions did nonetheless often effectively influence politics and public life by other means. Elite women patronized influential philosophers and political writers, the poor staged mass demonstrations in the streets to protest poor living conditions and bad government, and interest groups of various sorts circulated and submitted petitions, memorials, and protests. All of these forms of speech and action were both public and political in the pre-electoral age.

Public religious processions were yet another form of political commentary and action that lay outside the formal structures of civil government and politics, employed by both the formally and informally empowered alike. In an era when

---

1. This discussion of women's public activity refers to and draws particularly upon Linda K. Kerber, *No Constitutional Right to Be Ladies: Women and the Obligations of Citizenship* (New York: Hill and Wang, 1998); Kerber, *Women of the Republic: Intellect and Ideology in Revolutionary America* (New York: W. W. Norton, 1986); Joan B. Landes, *Women and the Public Sphere in the Age of the French Revolution* (Ithaca, NY: Cornell University Press, 1988); and Mary Ryan, *Women in Public: Between Banners and Ballots, 1825–1880* (Baltimore: Johns Hopkins University Press, 1990).

the separation of church and state was inconceivable to all but the most radical of nonconformists, civil rulers relied on the church's partnership to define the contours of political community and the sanctioned lines of power and authority. At the same time, while remaining within the approved format, processions could be used to stage alternative claims to authority by those who lacked official public power.

Processions communicated a message to a large public through the use of nonverbal, symbolic spectacle that required only a shared cultural vocabulary to be understood, a feature that made them particularly valuable in an age of limited literacy. The symbolism of a procession operated on several levels. Those who walked in it made a claim to their place in the community by traversing its physical space, thereby announcing themselves participants in sustaining the polity. The arrangement of various groups within the procession spoke to the power of each of these groups in relation to others in the defile. The closer an individual or group was to the most obviously important person in the procession, the more powerful they were understood to be. The route taken by a procession was equally meaningful. A procession that made its way across a town, passing the buildings that housed the highest-ranking officials of church and state and other spaces important to the well-being of the entire community, was more important than one that kept to a specific neighborhood, or simply took the shortest way between two points.[2]

2. Especially good discussions of early modern processions can be found in Barbara B. Diefendorf, *Beneath the Cross: Catholics and Huguenots in Sixteenth-*

Necessity dictated that there be some sort of Ursuline procession in 1734. When the Ursulines arrived in 1727, they were lodged in the town house of a wealthy concessionaire whose plantation was located upriver from New Orleans.[3] This was to serve as a temporary residence until the purpose-built convent promised them by the Company of the Indies could be constructed. Royal engineers drew up plans for a commodious building that included spaces for instruction, prayer, and lodging for the nuns and their students. Financial problems and the retrocession of the Louisiana colony to the French crown in 1731 delayed the project, and for seven years the nuns made do with a limited space ill-suited to their growing ministry. In addition to boarding students, day students, and large catechism classes for enslaved people, the temporary convent compound also served as the headquarters for an association of laywomen, known as a confraternity or congregation, called the Children of Mary, which was founded in 1730. The resources of the temporary convent were further strained by the acceptance of some thirty girls orphaned in an Indian attack on the French colonial outpost at Fort Rosalie, about a hundred miles upriver from New Orleans. When the permanent convent was completed in the summer of 1734, the nuns had to contemplate the best way to accomplish the physical transfer of the convent community. (See figs. 5 and 6.)

Century Paris (New York: Oxford University Press, 1991), 38–41; and Brian Pullan, *Rich and Poor in Renaissance Venice: The Social Institutions of a Catholic State, to 1620* (Cambridge, MA: Harvard University Press, 1971), 52, 59–60.

    3. Heaney, *Century of Pioneering*, 59.

The sisters could simply have had closed carriages transport them across the city to their new residence. This was the approach the New Orleans Ursulines took nearly two hundred years later in 1912, when they moved their convent for the third time. On that occasion, a public streetcar was chartered and its windows draped with black to shield the nuns, further concealed behind thick black veils, as they rode across the city. The Ursulines of 1734, however, opted for an explicitly public mode of transferring their community, and planned an elaborate procession designed to communicate clearly to the inhabitants of New Orleans the nuns' role in the community and the nature and quality of their authority.

The New Orleans nuns apparently modeled their procession, with its girls costumed as St. Ursula and her missionary companions, on a similar ceremony staged by the Ursuline nuns of Dijon when they moved into their convent in 1614. The colonial sisters read of the Dijon nuns' procession in a book carried with them from France, and borrowed liberally from its imagery to articulate the powerful spiritual authority that supported their mission. Like St. Ursula, the New Orleans Ursulines took their orders directly from God and persuaded fathers and other males who were their terrestrial superiors to step aside and allow them to do God's work. By making theirs a Eucharistic procession, the nuns announced their privileged position as custodians of their Lord's body: a consecrated host remained in a special receptacle on the altar of their convent chapel. The Ursulines also signaled the centrality of the sacrament of Holy Communion to the well-being of the entire population of the city, reminding the inhabitants that the sacrament bound them together into the body of God's church. The exclusion of nonclerical men from the processional ranks and the inclusion of the full social and racial spectrum of the city's women and girls, together with the procession's route past every major public landmark in the frontier capital, constituted other important elements of their processional message to colonial New Orleanians.[4] When the nuns closed their new convent gate behind them at the end of that summer's day in 1734 and resumed the physical invisibility dictated by their rule of cloister, they left the city's inhabitants with a powerful set of images to serve as reminders of their enduring presence and spiritual authority. The following account of the procession to the new convent on Saturday, July 17, 1734, was recorded by Sister Jeanne Melotte, who had left her French convent in 1732 to join the New Orleans Ursulines.[5]

EUCHARISTIC PROCESSION OF 1734

During the three days previous to the transfer to the new convent the weather seemed very unfavorable to this ceremony. Because of the continual rain which made the streets impassable, we were uncertain until two o'clock in the afternoon what

4. Marie-Augustine de Pommereu, *Les chroniques de l'ordre des Ursulines recueillies pour l'usage des religieuses du mesme ordre,* vol. 1, part 2 (Paris: Henault, 1673), 160–61.

5. The translation of the procession account is reprinted here verbatim from the translation prepared and published by Jane Frances Heaney in *Century of Pioneering,* 106–8.

to do. Then the sky cleared and we carried out the plans in spite of the mud that was so discouraging, especially for a group of some twenty young girls dressed as angels. One young girl representing St. Ursula was clothed in a robe of cloth of silver with a long train of the same material. Her hair was dressed with bands of pearls and diamonds and a small veil, the whole forming a superb crown. She held in her hand a heart pierced with an arrow. All was wrought with marvelous skill. Eleven young girls dressed in white and holding palms in their hands represented the eleven thousand virgins and accompanied St. Ursula. The little girls were angels.

At five o'clock in the evening we rang our two bells as a signal. Immediately, according to the order of Monsieur de Bienville, the Governor of Louisiana, the troops, both Swiss and French, began to march and drew up in order on both sides of our former house. The Reverend Jesuit and Capuchin Fathers, five in number (three Jesuits and two Capuchins) namely, Reverend Fathers de Beaubois and Le Petit and Brother Parisel, Reverend Fathers Philippe and Pierre, accompanied by quite a number of choir boys and chanters took their places in our chapel. Monsieurs Bienville, Governor, and Salmon, Intendant, honored us with their presence as did almost all the people of both the upper and lower classes of the city.

The Reverend Father Philippe, Capuchin curate of the parish, incensed the Blessed Sacrament. They sang some verses of the *Pange Lingua,* and, the Benediction having been given, the procession began to march. We went out in order wearing our choir mantles, with veils lowered and each carrying a lighted candle of white wax. The Mothers Superior and Assistant were near the Blessed Sacrament, which was carried under a rich canopy. The small community was composed of nine religious. The troops, drawn up on both sides of the street, marched in perfect order, single file, leaving between them and us a distance of about four feet. The drums and fifes accompanied the songs and made agreeable harmony. The citizens led the procession. Our day pupils followed. Our thirty orphans, each with a candle in her hand, formed a third group. Then came the ladies of the congregation, each with a lighted candle. There were about forty of these ladies. The community and the clergy terminated the procession. The order was well kept in spite of the mud and the singing of the children. No one got out of order as the Jesuit Brother Parisel, wearing a surplice, performed the office of master of ceremonies.

The procession entered the parish church where they had a reserved place for us in the sanctuary. The most Blessed Sacrament was placed on the altar and incensed. Then two soldiers wearing surplices and capes sang to music a motet to Ursula. This was followed by a beautiful sermon delivered by Reverend Father Le Petit of the Company of Jesus in which he showed that our establishment in this country was to the glory of God and the good of the colony. He praised our Institute very much for the education of youth.

As we left the church it was noticed that the troops were lined up, kneeling, holding the muzzles of their guns against the ground and bowing to adore the Most Blessed Sacrament. This ceremony was very respectful and devout. I thought, however, there was reason to fear that their interior sentiments were not in conformity with it.

Some persons had charged themselves to sound the bell of our new house; for these gentlemen had the kindness to give us one. As soon as they saw the procession approach, they rang it and did not cease until we had entered. The ceremony ended by benediction of the Blessed Sacrament, which we received in our inner chapel. From the moment we entered, the cloister was established.

As the next day was Sunday, we sang the Mass. The Blessed Sacrament was exposed and the *Te Deum* was chanted in thanksgiving. This had not been done the day before because it was late in the evening, and everyone was very much fatigued from the intense heat. Benediction of the Blessed Sacrament was given at five o'clock in the evening during which the Religious sang a most beautiful motet with music, which was appreciated by all the persons who assisted at the ceremony.

Three separate individuals supplied the English translation for the texts in this volume. The basic translation of Marie Madeleine Hachard's letters was completed by Sister Maria Dolores Hernandez, an Ursuline nun, now deceased, who held a Ph.D. from the University of Dijon, France. Hernandez worked from the original published version of the letters. Emily Clark edited Hernandez's translation and made some changes to it in an attempt to bring it closer to the more formal style of the eighteenth century. Although punctuation has been added for the sake of clarity, the rambling complex sentences of the original have been preserved when possible. Sylvia Probst, retired librarian at Ursuline Academy in New Orleans, provided a partially edited version of Hernandez's manuscript to Clark, which aided the process of final translation considerably.

The account of the 1734 procession was translated by Sister Jane Francis Heaney from the original contemporary manuscript account recorded in the "Délibérations du conseil" or convent chronicle. The manuscript volume is held by the Archives of the Ursuline Convent of New Orleans. Heaney's translation of the procession account has been previously published as a part of *A Century of Pioneering: A History of the Ursuline Nuns in New Orleans, 1727–1827*, originally a Ph.D. dissertation submitted to St. Louis University in 1949 and privately published by the Ursuline Sisters of New Orleans as a monograph in 1993.

The obituary letters were translated by Emily Clark, primarily from the eighteenth-century originals contained in the manuscript volume entitled "Lettres circulaires," held in the Archives of the Ursuline Convent of New Orleans. Some of the pages in this volume are badly deteriorated. In some cases, parts of pages are in fragments; in others, poor quality, caustic ink has rendered large passages illegible. Presumably it was in response to this deterioration that a decision was made at some point in the nineteenth century to make a new manuscript copy of the obituary letters. The copyist edited and abridged the letters. In some cases the editing was clearly in response to illegible passages, but there is also a pattern of shortening the descriptions of deathbed scenes. In cases where portions of the original eighteenth-century manuscript are missing or illegible, Clark relied on the nineteenth-century manuscript copy, which is also held by the Archives of the Ursuline Convent of New Orleans.

The spelling of the names of individuals and places, which sometimes vary within a single manuscript document from one passage to the next, has been standardized throughout this edition.

PUBLICATION HISTORY OF HACHARD'S LETTERS

FRENCH EDITIONS

1728 Hachard, Marie Madeleine. *Relation du voyage des dames religieuses Ursulines de Roüen à la Nouvelle-Orléans, parties de France le 22 février 1727 et arrivez à La Louisienne le 23 juillet de la même année.* Rouen: A. Le Prévost, 1728.

1865 Hachard, Marie Madeleine. *Relation du voyage des religieuses Ursulines de Rouen a la Nouvelle-Orléans en 1727, et précédée d'une notice par Paul Baudry.* Rouen: H. Boissel, 1865.

1872 Hachard, Marie Madeleine. *Relation du voyage des dames religieuses Ursulines de Rouen a la Nouvelle-Orleans, avec une introduction et des notes par Gabriel Gravier.* Paris, Maisonneuve, 1872.

1988 Hachard, Marie Madeleine. *De Rouen à la Louisiane: voyage d'une Ursuline en 1727.* Foreword by J.-P. Chaline. Rouen: Association d'études normandes, 1988.

ENGLISH TRANSLATIONS

1925 [Wolfe, Mother Thérèse]. *The Ursulines in New Orleans and Our Lady of Prompt Succor: A Record of Two Centuries, 1727–1925.* Edited by Henry Churchill Simple. New York: P. J. Kennedy & Sons, 1925.

1940 Hachard, Marie Madeleine. *Voyage of the Ursuline Nuns to New Orleans, translated from the French of Gabriel Gravier by Olivia Blanchard.* New Orleans: Survey of Federal Archives in Louisiana, 1940.

1974 Hachard, Marie Madeleine. *The Letters of Marie Madeleine Hachard, 1727–28.* Translated by Myldred Masson Costa. New Orleans: [s.n.], 1974.

CPSIA information can be obtained
at www.ICGtesting.com
Printed in the USA
LVHW011834020419
612711LV00017B/275/P